Creative Keyboard Presents

JAZZ PIANO CHORDS

By Misha V. Stefanuk

1 2 3 4 5 6 7 8 9 0

Creative Keyboard Publications MEL BAY

CHECK OUT CREATIVE KEYBOARD'S FREE WEBZINE @ www.creativekeyboard.com

Visit us on the Web at www.melbay.com — E-mail us at email@melbay.com

Preface

The piano is a unique instrument. More notes can be played simultaneously on the piano than on any other instrument. Piano chords have more sounds and are more complex than chords for other instruments. My intention in writing this book is to create something I would like to have and use myself.

Credits

I want to thank my wife Evan Marie Dozier-Stefanuk for her help in writing this book. I would also like to mention the names of my teachers: John Arnn, Jeff Kirk, William Pursell, Frank Mantooth, Charles Argersinger, Greg Yasinitsky, Urij Kozirev, Larisa Pashanova, and Dmitry Blum.

Table of Contents

Intervals

The distance between two pitches is called an interval. The smallest interval in the well-tempered system that is playable on the piano is called the half step. Every other interval can be measured in half steps. Another measuring device is called a whole step and it is equal to two half steps. The name of each interval is made up of two parts, the interval degree and its modifier. First, the degree of the interval must be determined by counting pitches by letter (including the starting pitch as one.) For instance, C to D is a second, C to E is a third, etc. Although you can't play two of the same pitch on the piano the way you can on some instruments, that interval is called a Unison.

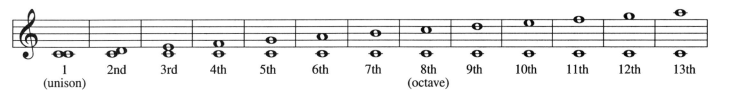

Second, modifiers determine an interval's quality compared to intervals derived from the major scale:

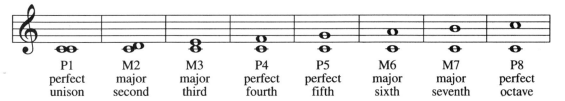

Other interval modifiers are: augmented (one half step more then major or perfect):

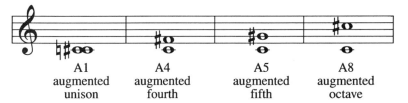

minor (one half step less than major):

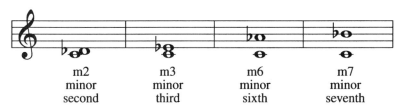

diminished (one half step less then perfect or minor):

(although minor intervals that are lowered one half step are also diminished, you will probably only see the diminished 7th used often):

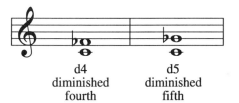

When you raise the lower of two pitches in an interval up an octave (or lower the upper pitch one octave), you have created an **inversion**. When you compare an interval with it's inversion, the intervals are called **complementary,** and are close in tone quality and function:

Traditionally, intervals were divided into consonant and dissonant, where dissonant intervals tend to gravitate toward consonant ones.

The **consonant intervals** are:

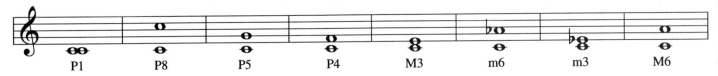

Dissonant intervals create the feeling of tension that needs resolving.

The **dissonant intervals** are:

Dissonant intervals have a tendency to resolve to consonant intervals as follows:

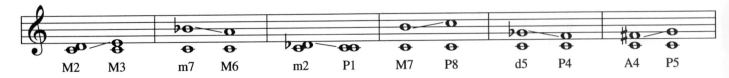

The simplest resolution is when the dissonant sound of the interval resolves into the closest consonant (half step rather then a whole step):

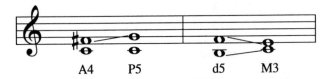

When we hear a note that sounds like a single pitch, there are in fact several pitches blending with that note. The primary pitch is called the **Fundamental**, and the other pitches that are sounding are called **Overtones** or **Harmonics**. What we perveive as the tone or timbre of a note, are the fundamental and the various overtones sounding at different volumes relative to each other. Different balances within the overtones result in different timbres. In the following example, C (two octaves below Middle C) is the fundamental.

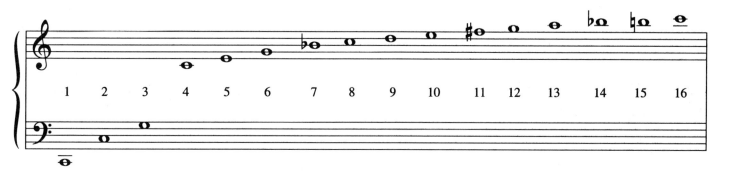

Intervals increase in dissonance following the order in the overtone series. The more dissonant intervals are less stable and require a resolution into more consonant.

- **P1**   **P8**   very consonant
- **P5**   **P4**
- **M3**   **m6**
- **m3**   **M6**
- **M2**   **m7**
- **m2**   **M7**
- **tritone**   very dissonant

Compound intervals are intervals bigger than the octave:

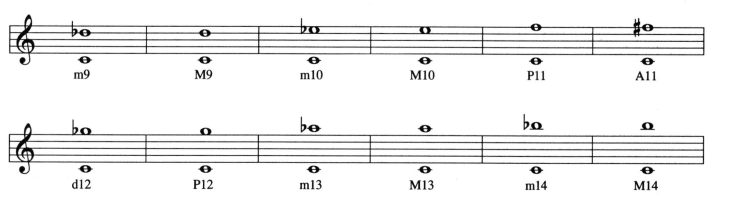

7

There is a specific way to refer to compound intervals in jazz due to the spelling of complex chords, such as 9th, 11th, and 13th. It is common to call notes raised or lowered from their positions in the major scale as ♯ and ♭, regardless of how they fall in the key that they are used in. In the chord B7, the fifth is F♯, but with a lowered fifth, the chord is called B7(♭5), and not B7(♮5).

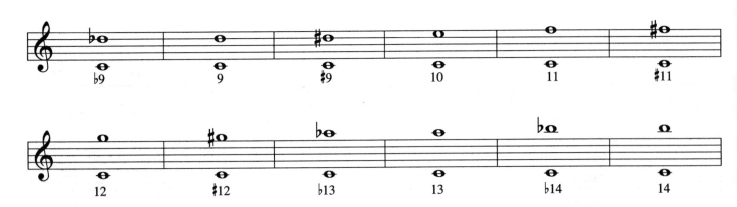

Enharmonic spelling of a pitch is a way to name the same pitch differently. For example: C♯ is the same pitch as D♭, and E♯ is the same pitch as F. When deciding which enharmonic to use, just count the number of letters in the interval that you want. The pitches B and G make the sound of an augmented fifth, but their letter names are a sixth apart. Because F♯ is a perfect fifth from B, you would raise F♯ to F♯♯ (written as F✗) for a true augmented fifth.

Enharmonic intervals suggest quite different resolution. For example:

The first and the last groups in the next example show that sometimes the dissonant interval resolves into another dissonant interval, which will finally resolve into a consonant. Also resolution in the first group is more dictated by the voice leading than by acoustic tension:

Notes belonging to the Major or minor scale are called **diatonic**:

Major   Natural Minor

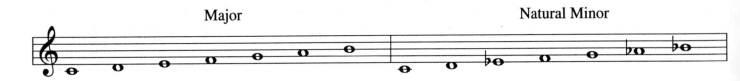

8

Notes not belonging to the scale are called **non-scale tones**:

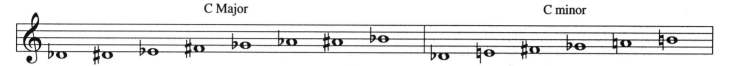

Chromatic tones have a tendency to resolve into the closest diatonic notes, sometimes going against the simplest resolution of the interval not being considered in the tonal context:

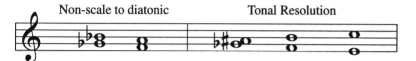

Notes moving by half-step up or down the piano belong to the **Chromatic Scale**:

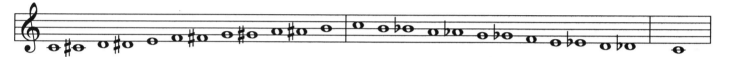

The two **tritones** found amongst diatonic intervals (**d5** and **A4**) both have a very strong resolutions into stable "tonic" intervals:

Chords

A **chord** is a combination of 3 or more pitches. The most common chord is a **triad**, a combination of two thirds. **A triad** has 2 inversions:

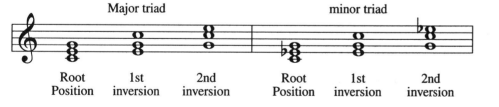

There are six different triads widely used in jazz music:

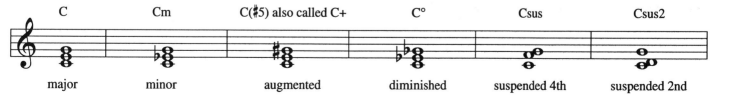

9

Major and minor triads are the most stable chords in tonal music. However in jazz music of the second half of the twentieth century, the major triad as a pure chord is usually avoided. The sonority of the chord sounds too simple and also brings the feeling of pop music with it. The **CMaj** symbol in a contemporary score rarely means the C major triad.

An **augmented** triad is a very unstable chord, strongly needing a resolution. The sound of the chord is confusing due to a symmetrical structure which makes inversions of the chord equal:

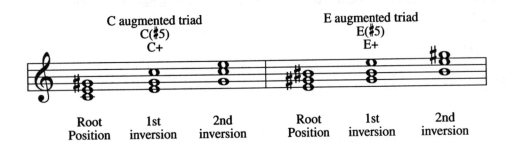

A **diminished** triad has some of the same qualities with an augmented triad, but becomes totally symmetrical only as a 7th chord:

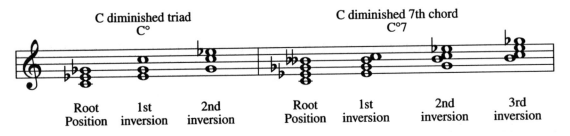

Traditionally suspended chords needed resolution (the fourth or second resolving to the third), but in modern context they can be considered a temporary tonic, replacing a major or minor chord in function. The suspended 4th is more common than the suspended 2nd. Because of this, the '4' is usually left off, leaving (for example) B♭sus, instead of B♭sus4. Suspended 2nd is written out as B♭sus2.

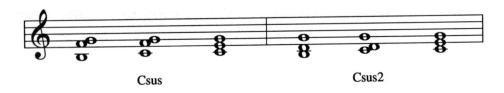

A **6th chord** is built by starting with a triad, and adding the pitch that is a sixth from the root. The two minor 6th chords are less stable than the Major one:

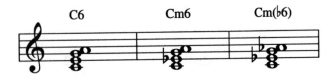

7th chords are among the most used chords in jazz music. Two main characteristics of the sound of the chord are **relative stability** and **color**. The degree of stability depends on the amount of tension of the intervals of the chord. Stability is also affected by the voice leading. Color refers to the emotional effect the chord by itself has on a listener. Tension deals with the dynamic process of moving from one chord to another, while the color is a static quality of each individual chord.

There are four types of seventh chords; **Dominant, Major, Minor and Diminished**.

One of the most frequently used of the 7th chords are called **Dominant chords**. The name 'dominant' comes from the seventh chord that is built on the fifth degree of the major scale (the so-called dominant note). Traditionally, the dominant chord had an unstable sound, that was usually resolved into the first chord of the key (also called the 'tonic'). An example of this is G7 to C in the key of C. Because jazz and blues both evolved in similar settings and borrow from each other, the practice in blues of using a dominant chord in a tonic function is common in jazz also. Dominant chords contain the intervals of a major third and a minor seventh. The exception to this is the sus chord, which in jazz can be used in place of chords with major or minor thirds in some cases.

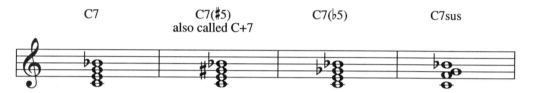

Seventh chords that have a major third and a major seventh are called **Major Seventh**. The sus exception may be applied here as well.

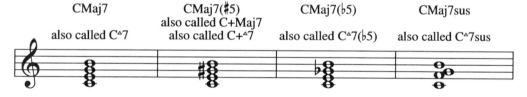

Seventh chords that have a minor third and a minor seventh are called **Minor Seventh**. A related chord is the **Minor Major Seventh**, which has a minor third and a major seventh. The minor major seventh chord functions similarly to the minor seventh chord.

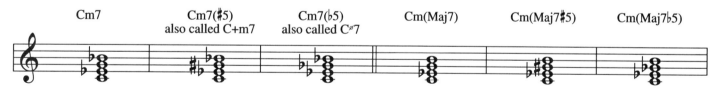

The last type of seventh chord is the **Diminished Seventh** chord. It has a minor third, diminished fifth, and diminished seventh. Although the diminished seventh interval is enharmonically the same pitch as the major sixth, it needs to be written as a diminished seventh, because chords are primarily written in thirds. Although it has a minor third, it's function is less like the minor seventh type chords, and is a unique chord unto itself.

9th, 11th and 13th chords are widely used in jazz music. They are the reason jazz harmony is so different in sound from pop or earlier (pre 20th century) classical. 9th, 11th and 13th chords are built by adding upper scale-tones to seventh chords, and can be major, minor, or dominant, depending on the type of the seventh chord that they are built on. In jazz, you could use a 9th, 11th or 13th chord in most situations where you would use a seventh chord. There are many variations on these chords, but telling what type of chord you have is determined by a few simple rules. These rules pertain to the notes that make up the chords, and not necessarily to the notes of the chord that you choose for your voicing.

1. A 9th chord needs a seventh. A triad with a ninth but no seventh is a separate kind of chord called an add9 (root, third, fifth, ninth). C add9 is similar to Csus2 (because the second and the ninth are enharmonically the same pitch), except that the sus2 chord has no third (the 2 acts as the third, suspended below). In theory, you could have an add11 (1, 3, 5, 11), an add13 (1, 3, 5, 13), or any combination of 9, 11 & 13 without a seventh, but in reality you may never see anything beyond an add9.

2. An 11th chord needs a third. Because the fourth and the eleventh are the same pitch, the only way to tell them apart is the presence of the third. Without a third, the chord will sound like a sus, but with a third it takes on the sound of the 11th. Major chords usually use a raised 11th ($\sharp11$), while minor chords are more likely to use the diatonic 11th.

3. A 13th chord needs a seventh. Because the sixth and the thirteenth are the same pitch, the only way to tell them apart is the presence of the seventh. Without a seventh, the chord is a 6th chord, but with a seventh it is 13th. If you have a sixth and a ninth without a seventh, that is a separate kind of chord called a six-nine chord (usually written C$\frac{6}{9}$). The six-nine chord, like the sixth chord, works well in situations where you would use a major chord.

Piano Chords

The way a pianist plays chords depends on the function of the instrument at the time. There are five distinct functions that a piano can serve:

- accompaniment for a soloist – bass line and chords
- accompaniment for a soloist in a piano trio (with a bass player) – chords in both hands low range
- accompaniment for a bass solo – chords in both hands
- solo with piano trio – left hand chords
- solo without bass – bass line and chords in the left hand

These parameters bring certain limitations to the way a chord should be played. The first and the most important rule is that a **chord should not be in the way**. The bottom note of a chord should be out of the typical range of the bass player if there is one. The top notes should be almost out of range of the soloist, or a complementary rhythm should be used for comping. When the soloing instrument is in the middle range of the keyboard, like baritone saxophone for example, the pianist needs to be very careful not to "bury" the soloist. It is always better to **play less than to play more**. However when there is no bass player, the piano takes over the bass register, and has to create a harmonic foundation for the whole piece. This can be accomplished by playing accompaniment textures like rag time, boogie woogie, walking bass line, repetitive figures in the left hand and so on. Other considerations for the voicing of a chord are color, tension and comfort for the pianist.

Four Way Close Voicing

The simplest voicing of the chord is **four way close voicing**:

Open Voicing

The voicing that allows open spaces between the sounds is called an **open position**. It provides a very clean, full and open sound:

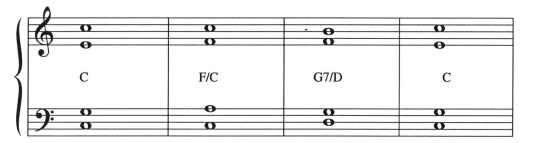

Drop Voicing

The first problem that needs to be solved is finding the bass note of the chord. It is a common understanding that playing the same note as the bass player is not the best decision. The simplest and oldest tool for this is a **drop-2** voicing widely used by arrangers. The method of writing **drop-2** is very simple. The 2nd note from the bottom of **four way close** voicing needs to be played an octave down. The sound of the resulting chord is more colorful, more interesting and more typical for jazz playing:

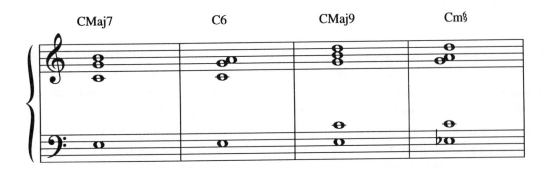

Another useful tool is a **drop-3**, which is very similar to drop-2:

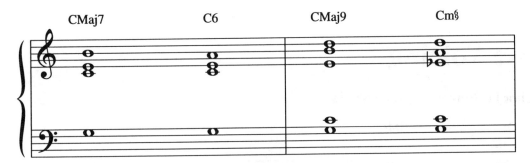

Left Hand Voicings

The main objective for the left hand voicings is to avoid a busy texture. The acoustics of the piano makes close intervals in the middle low range sound "mushy" and unclear. Unless there is a specific sound effect to be achieved, excess use of intervals less than a third should be avoided.

Three and Four Note Voicing

Three note voicings are mostly used in the left hand while playing solo with a bass player. The chord degrees are treated quite differently in jazz music. The degrees that should always appear in the chord are 3rd and 7th. The 5th of the chord is often dropped unless altered. To avoid the interruption with a bass player the tonic should not be played. All higher voicings can be a part of the chord but are not necessary. The **3 note voicing** provides a safe foundation for bringing upper voicings in the right hand. A very important concept in playing chords in jazz is **the concept of the voice leading** — when every note of the chord travels to the closest note of the next chord.

An example of the **3 note voicing**:

Use of the four way close voicings in the left hand provides slightly more complex sound:

Fourth (Quartal) Voicing

A very modern sound is produced by the chords containing two perfect fourths:

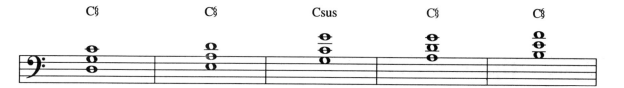

The very identifiable sound of the 4th combined with a functional bass line and added solo line creates a multifunctional open structure sound. The concept of **fourth voicing** comes from **modal harmony** where the chords are derived from the scale being used.

Root and Seventh Voicing

Despite the usual avoidance of the root in the bass, one widely used left hand voicing idea is playing the root and the 7th of the chord only:

Usually the right hand plays the rest of the chord, but sometimes the root and 7th stand alone. It is important to mention that this voicing is perfect for playing when there is no bass player. The open sound structures of the left hand provide basis for upper voicings of the right hand and a solo line.

Third and Seventh Voicing

This is very close to root and 7th concept. You can also add the 9th or other upper voicings, avoiding excessive busyness in texture. In a dominant chord this creates a tritone — the unstable interval that is the main characteristic of the dominant chord itself:

Blues Chord

There are two chords that are lifesavers for dominant harmonies. The first one is made of the 3rd, dominant 7th, and altered 9th, and the second is made of the Dominant 7th, 3rd, and 13th. The structure of these two chords is similar, and they alone provide the basis for the whole blues progression with the correct voice leading:

Right-Hand Upper Voicings

The building of a chord with its foundation in the left hand can be greatly improved by the right-hand upper structures. Even though the function of the chord is fairly clear from the bass and the left hand, the sonority and color of the chord can vary dramatically by added pitches in the right hand.

Ninth, Eleventh, and Thirteenth

Ninth, eleventh, and thirteenth are usually called tensions or alterations. The following example shows full 13th chords, the left hand 1st and 7th, as well as 3rd and 7th concepts:

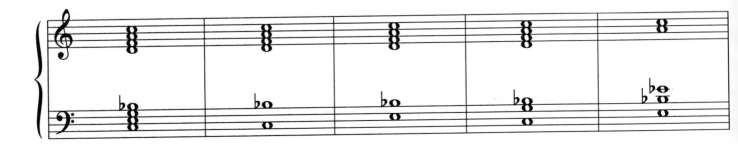

The last chord is based on the "blues" chord and does not contain 9th or 11th in the right hand because altered 9th is present in the left hand.

Polychords/Triads as Upper Voicings

Some altered chords can also be written as a combination of two chords — a **polychord**. This way of transcribing a functional chord calls for almost exact note choice and simplifies the reading process:

• C9	• Gm/C
• Cm9	• Gm/Cm
• CMaj9	• G/C
• Cm9(Maj7)	• G/Cm
• C7(♯9)	• E♭/C
• CMaj7(♯11)	• B♭(♯5)/C
• Cm11	• B♭/Cm
• C13	• Dm/C7
• Cm13	• Dm/Cm7
• C13(♯11)	• D/C7
• C7(♭9♯11)	• F♯/C
• C7(♯5♯9)	• A♭/C7
• C13(♭9)	• A/C7
• C7(♯5♭9)	• D♭/C7
• CMaj7(♯5)	• E/C*
• C13sus	• F/C7

* don't voice a fifth in the C chord

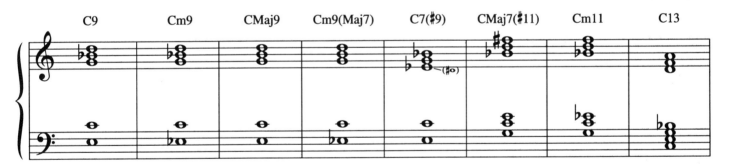

17

The right hand part can be used in any inversion as well as the left hand:

C13(♯11)* C13(♯11)* C13(♯11)* C13(♯11) C13(♯11) C13(♯11)

This way of thinking makes chord reading much faster and precise when applicable.

C13(♯5♭9)* C13(♯11)* Cm7 CMaj7(♯5) C13sus

C7(♭9♯11)* CMaj9* C7(♯5♯9)* C13(♭9) C7sus

The same rules apply to minor triads in the right hand:

• Cm7	• Cm/C7‡
• C7(♯5♭9)	• C♯m/C7
• C13sus	• Dm/C7
• C(♯9♯11)	• D♯m/C7
• C11♭13	• Fm/C7
• C7sus(♭9)	• B♭m/C7
• Cm7(♭5)	• E♭m/C7‡
• C13(♭9♯11)	• F♯m/C7
• C9	• Gm/C7
• C13	• Am/C7

‡ don't voice a fifth in left hand

* Chord voiced without a 3rd.

18

Suspended Fourth Voicings

Suspended fourth voicings can also be built as polychords

• 9sus	• Bb/C7*	
• 9sus	• Gm/C7*	
• 13sus	• Dm/C7*	
• 13sus	• F/C7*	
• 7sus(#5b9)	• Db/C7*	

* don't voice a third in left hand

A more complex sound can be achieved by using 7th chords in the right hand:

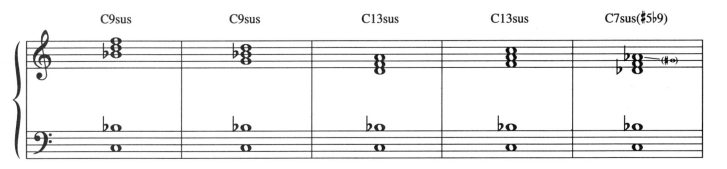

* Because this chord has a third, it is no longer a sus chord.

19

Another way to build sus chords would be a polychord containing two sus structures:

• 9sus	• D7sus/C7sus
• 7sus(#5#9)	• E♭7sus/C7sus
• 7sus(#9)	• F7sus/C7sus
• 7sus	• G7sus/C7sus
• 7sus(#5#9)	• B♭7sus/C7sus

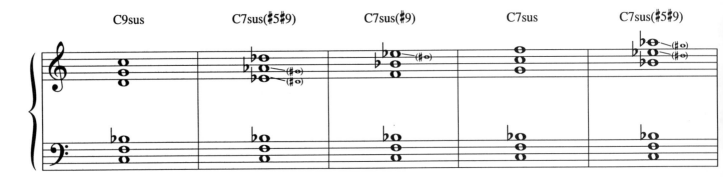

All-Four Voicings

Chords that contain all 4ths in both hands create a tense, modern jazz sound and are often use in a **modal** context:

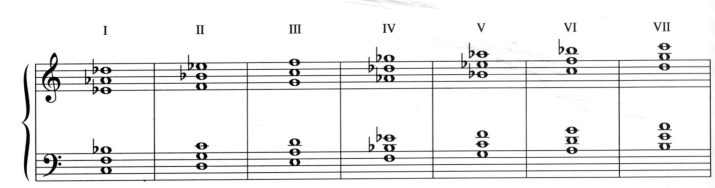

Notice that only II and VII really belong to the C major and all the rest are C minor chords. Functionally these are hard to catalog. There are also endless combinations of the four voicings mixed with other chords. Sometimes an all-4 voicing can be put on the top of the functional chord without greatly affecting its functional quality:

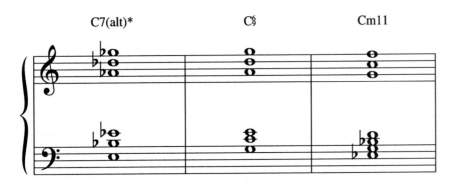

* This voicing has a very quartal sound, and because of it's many altered pitches, can be used in many situations. Notice that it contains both raised and lowered ninths. Also, depending on which enharmonic pitch you want to call some notes, raised eleventh or lowered fifth, and raised fifth or lowered thirteenth.

Alterations of the Upper Voicings

Every voice in the upper voicings has a tendency to resolve. In a basic 13th chord, the 7th goes down to the 6th, the 9th can go either down to the tonic or up to the 3rd, the 11th resolves to the 3rd or the 5th, and the 13th goes down to the 5th:

Upper Voicing	Resolves into
• 7th	• 6th
• 9th	• tonic or 3rd
• 11th	• 3rd or 5th
• 13th	• 5th

Alterations of the basic upper voicings can make these tensions stronger and make the sound of the chord more interesting. As a rule, the altered voice resolves in the direction of the alteration:

Alteration	Resolves in
• ♭9	• Tonic
• ♯9	• 3rd
• ♯11	• 5th
• ♭13	• 5th
• ♯13	• Major 7th, then tonic

Split Ninth Chords

Occasionally, chords with both forms of altered 9th occur. Both of the altered 9ths have very strong tension, resulting in a highly chromatic chord:

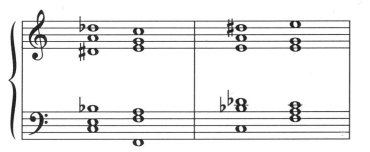

21

Function of Chords in a Key

Most jazz music and jazz harmony has a tonal foundation that it is based on one or more keys. This makes it possible to analyze chords in a tonal context. Each pitch of the scale calls for a chord structure:

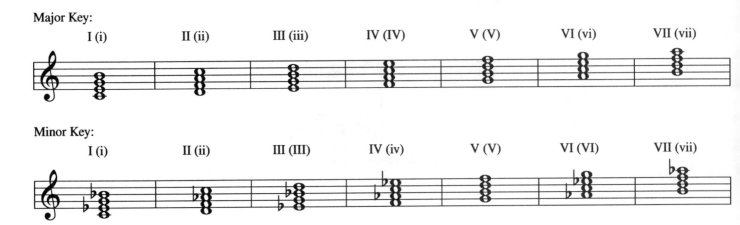

The diatonic chords based on the notes of the scale serve different functions. The strongest ones are I, IV, and V, so called **tonic**, **subdominant**, and **dominant**. **Tonic** (I) chords are very stable and serve as arrival and departure points. **Dominant** (V) is the strongest tense chord and it resolves to I. **Dominant** chord is always a Major chord with minor 7th, if a 7th is present. **Subdominant** (IV) moves to the dominant chord. II serves as a subdominant, III as an unstable (temporary) tonic, VI can be a **temporary tonic** or **subdominant**, and VII is called a **leading chord** and serves the function of an alternative dominant. The **leading VII** chord in minor is built on the altered ♯7th.

Alternative Bass

Sometimes the top portion of the chord is complete but the bass is looked upon as an independent unit with its own resolutions:

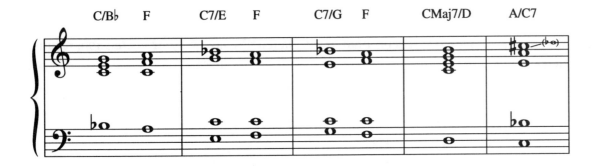

The first three chords in the example above are just inversions of the 7th chord written very precisely. The CMaj7/D chord is a true polychord that might not need resolution since its counterparts are rather stable. The A/C7 chord can be notated as C13(♭9) and is a very attractive form of the dominant chord.

Another function polychords can serve is making a simple harmonic structure more sophisticated:

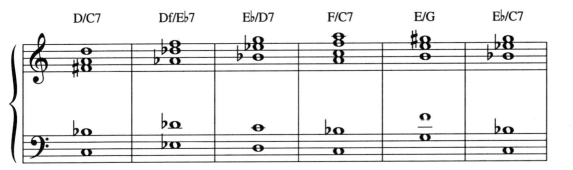

The left hand in this example does not sound very attractive by itself, but the **polychordal upper voicings** make it much more appealing.

Substitution

Chords can be replaced by other chords that are close in function and/or sonority. There are a number of the **substitutions** that can be used. The first one is a **3ʳᵈ substitution**, when the chord is replaced by another chord which is a 3ʳᵈ up or down from the original in the same key:

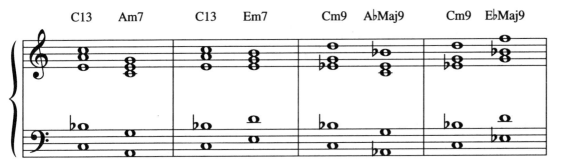

Another common substitution is a **tritone substitution**:

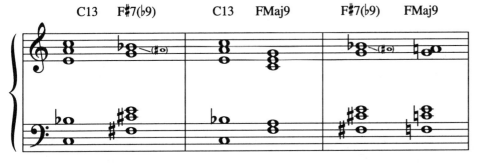

Substitutions are based on the common tones of the chords or similar functions that they serve. Notice that in the last pair there is a **parallel fifth** between the bottom two voices, which is considered a mistake in classical voice leading. However in Jazz music altered parallel chords with fifths and octaves are common.

Substitutions can be used either instead of the original chord, or with it:

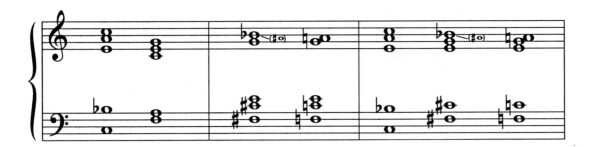

The objective of **substitution** is to make the harmony more interesting and colorful. Obviously the slower the tempo the more freedom the pianist has to alter chords or substitute them. However extreme caution has to be used when making sudden alterations of the harmony. Jazz is a collective conversational art. Some changes are rather safe while others can confuse other members of the band, creating unexpected and unwanted dissonance between different alterations being played simultaneously and being destructive to the resulting sound. Musical taste and common sense will be developed as a result of using alterations and substitutions.

The next type of **substitution** is when the chord is replaced by a **group of chords**, usually not more than 3. Often those chords are in dominant or subdominant-dominant relation with the original chord:

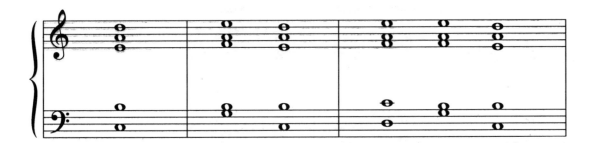

Chords used for this kind of substitution can also be altered and substituted:

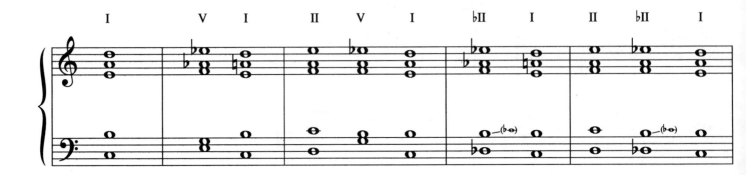

Notice the misspelling in the second and fourth bar due to the voice leading.

A very interesting combination would be substituting the dominant chord with a tritone substitution and then substituting the tritone substitution with a dominant-tonic progression:

(key of F)

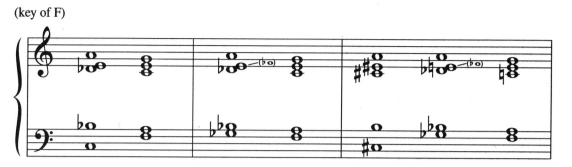

Changing of the chord structure usually is used to create more tension toward the next chord:

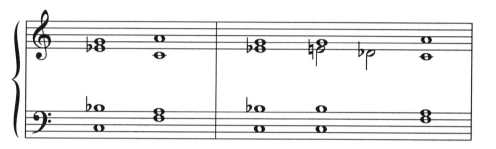

This type of substitution uses a concept of secondary dominant chords. Sometimes this creates a temporary tonic, strengthening the chord by exposing its dominant or subdominant-dominant counterparts:

The last example has a pause inserted in it to accent the effect of the temporary tonic in F before it. Another common substitution technique is bringing a chord a half step up or down before the original chord:

Clusters

Chords made of seconds are called **clusters**. Usually **clusters** are based on playing all notes of the scale in the given range:

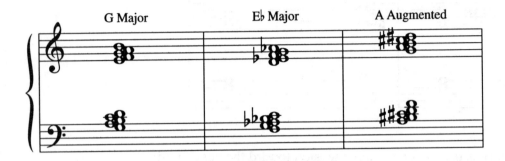

Clusters can be modified and combined with other voicings:

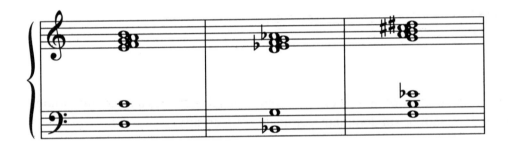

One way to alter clusters is to use a **drop 2** or **drop 3** voicing, very similar to the traditional **drop 2**:

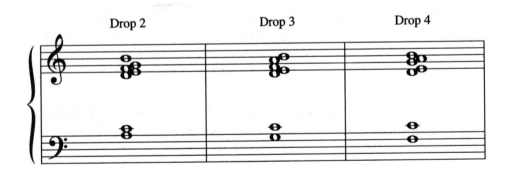

Polytonal Clusters

Polytonal clusters contain two or more easily identifiable separate scale units, like Major scale from C to G in the left hand and pentatonic scale from E♭ to B♭ in the right hand, etc:

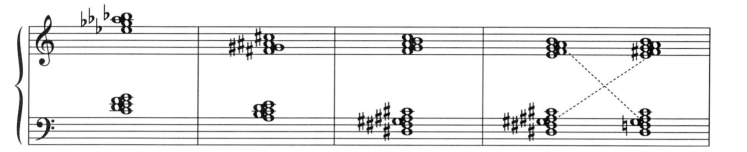

The last chord also combines the **drop 4** and **drop 2** technique.

Another way of looking at the clusters is to analyze each sound of the cluster as an altered note from a triad-based chord:

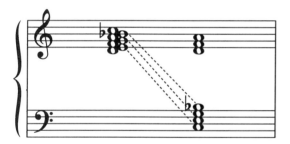

Sometimes clusters are also used as upper structures to embellish the functional basic chord:

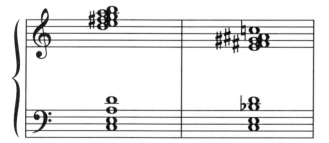

The first chord is a combination of a standard C6, very characteristic of C Major tonic chord, and a cluster made from the lydian scale. Functionally, the result is a very stable Major tonic chord. The second example consists of a C7(♭9) and a cluster made of augmented scale. The result is clearly a chord of dominant function.

Block Chords

Chords built down from the melody note are called **block chords**. A **block chord** is not a specific type of chord but the way a chord is built from the linear movement of the voices. They are derived from the technique of writing for ensemble of instruments playing the tune. The top instrument plays the melody and all the rest of them follow in a parallel motion but using mostly chord tones. When the top voice uses **non-chord tones**, so do other voices:

Notice that functionally chords can go the "wrong" direction because every voice is following the top voice line. One of the common practices is to double the melody in the left hand an octave lower than the original melody:

Chord Function

Chords can have very different functions. **Major and minor** chords usually are **stable** and do not have a strong tendency to resolve into another chord. However, functionally they can play the subdominant role and enhance the tension-resolution of the dominant-tonic group. **Dominant** chords almost always have **strong tensions** to be resolved into a chord a fifth lower, except for the case discussed below. **Diminished** chords are not stable but may have many different ways to resolve. **Suspended 2 and 4** chords can be stable or can be **dominant** depending on the musical context. **Alteration** of the chord can make the tension to resolve either stronger or weaker, and the resulting chord will become more stable as an independent identity. **Polychords** can be very **dominant**, take **dominant/tonic** for example, but can also be very stable although often with neither Major nor minor quality easily detectable:

Chord Quality	Tonal Function in Major	Tonal Function in minor
• Major	• I, IV	• III, VI
• Minor	• II, III, IV, VI	• I, IV
• Dominant	• V, VII	• V, VII
• Diminished	• VII	• II, ♯VI, ♯VII

The position of a chord in a key often defines the role the chord plays in the piece:

Chord	Function
• I M	• Establishing the Major Key
• I m	• Establishing the minor Key
• I 7	• Tension towards IV or VI
• ♭II	• Substitution for V7, tension towards I
• II m	• Tension towards V or ♭II
• II	• Tension towards V or ♭II
• ♭III	• Substitution for VI, tension towards II or ♭VI
• III m	• Substitution for I, tension towards ♭III or VI
• III	• Substitution for I, tension towards ♭III or VI
• IV m	• Tension towards V or I
• IV M	• Temporary tonic, tension towards V or I
• V	• Tension towards I or VI
• VI m	• Tension towards II
• VI M	• Tension towards II or ♭VI
• ♭VI	• Tension towards I/V or V
• VII	• Tension towards I or VI
• ♭VII	• Tension towards V or II

Dominant chords can also have a different enharmonic spelling and resolve differently following the "new" tensions of the "new" spelling. The classical example of the wrong resolution of the **dominant 7th** chord is so called **augmented 6th chord** that resolves into **I/V** chord of the key, a Major third higher than the original:

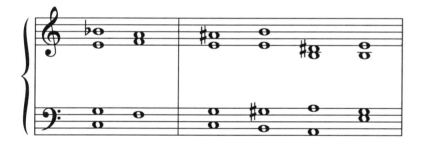

Another example of an unusual resolution would be resolving the augmented triad a half step up instead of the usual resolution as a dominant to a Tonic:

The following chord charts are divided in **Major, minor, Dominant, diminished** and **sustained** and also have a special section dedicated to **4th based** chord sonorities. This way of cataloging chords can be helpful, but sometimes chords can have a function other than suggested.

These charts can be very helpful for practicing and for quick and easy reference to which chords are best for harmonizing. It is important to remember that they are mostly a learning tool used to develop harmonic thinking and feeling in all keys, and may not cover every possibility.

The **Chord Charts** consist of chords available for specific bass notes.
The **Melody Harmonization Charts** are designed to help in finding different harmonization for any given note.
The **Quartal Harmonies Charts** consist of 4th based chords.
The **Spelling Suggestions Chart**: Many chord symbols acquired a number of different spellings. The spelling suggestions chart consists of different spellings for chords.

The following charts do not include the different **substitutions**, but those can be found by using the charts. For example to replace a **C7** chord, the first step might be to find a **tritone substitute**, which would be F#. The next step might be to choose the Dominant chord in F# and make sure that it does not have tensions that go against the tensions marked in the original chord:

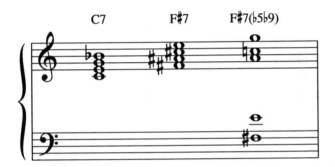

Making choices in harmonization of melodic lines utilizes knowledge, experience and taste. It also shows artistic personality and is one of the keys to develop a personal style.

Chords-Key of C

Major Chords

CMaj7 · CMaj7 · CMaj7 · CMaj7 · CMaj7(♯5) · CMaj9 · CMaj9 · CMaj9

CMaj9 · CMaj9 · CMaj9 · CMaj9 · CMaj9 · CMaj9 · C$_9^6$ · C$_9^6$

C$_9^6$ · C$_9^6$(♯11) · C$_9^6$(♯11) · C$_9^6$(♯11) · C$_9^6$(♯11) · C$_9^6$ · CMaj13 · CMaj13

Minor Chords

Cm7 · Cm7 · Cm7 · Cm7 · Cm7 · Cm7 · Cm9 · Cm9

Cm9 · Cm9 · Cm9 · Cm9 · Cm9 · Cm add9 · Cm11 · Cm11

Chords-Key of C

| Cm11 | Cm11 | Cm11 | Cm11 | Cm6 | Cm6 | Cm9(6) | Cm9(6) |

Dominant Chords

| Cm9(6) | Cm(Maj7) | Cm9(Maj7) | Cm9(Maj7) | C7 | C7 | C7 | C7(♯5) |

| C7(♯5) | C7(♯5) | C7(♭5) | C7(♭5) | C9 | C9 | C9 | C7(♭9) |

| C7(♭9) | C7(♭9) | C7(♭9) | C13(♭9) | C7(♯5,♭9) | C7(♭9) | C7(♭5,♭9) | C7(♭5,♭9) |

| C7(♭5,♭9) | C7(♭5,♭9) | C7(♯9) | C7(♯5,♭9) | C7(♯9) | C7(♯5,♭9) | C7(♯5,♭9) | C11 |

Chords-Key of C

| C7($^{\sharp5}_{\sharp9\sharp11}$) | C7($\sharp$11) | C9($\sharp$11) | C13($\sharp$11) | C13sus | C13sus | C13 | C13 |

Diminished Chords

| C13 | C13 | C13 | C13 | C13($\flat$9) | C13($\sharp$11) | Cm7($\flat$5) | Cm7($\flat$5) |

| Cm7($\flat$5) | Cm11($\flat$5) | C°7 | C°Maj7 | Cm9($\flat$5) | Cm11($\flat$5) | Cm11($\flat$5) |

Suspended Chords

| Cadd9 | C$^6_9$ | Csus2 | Csus | Csus | Csus2 | C9sus | C9sus | C9sus |

| C9sus | C9sus($\flat$5) | D/C | D/C | B$\flat$/C | B$\flat$/C | F/C | F/C |

33

Chords-Key of D♭

Major Chords

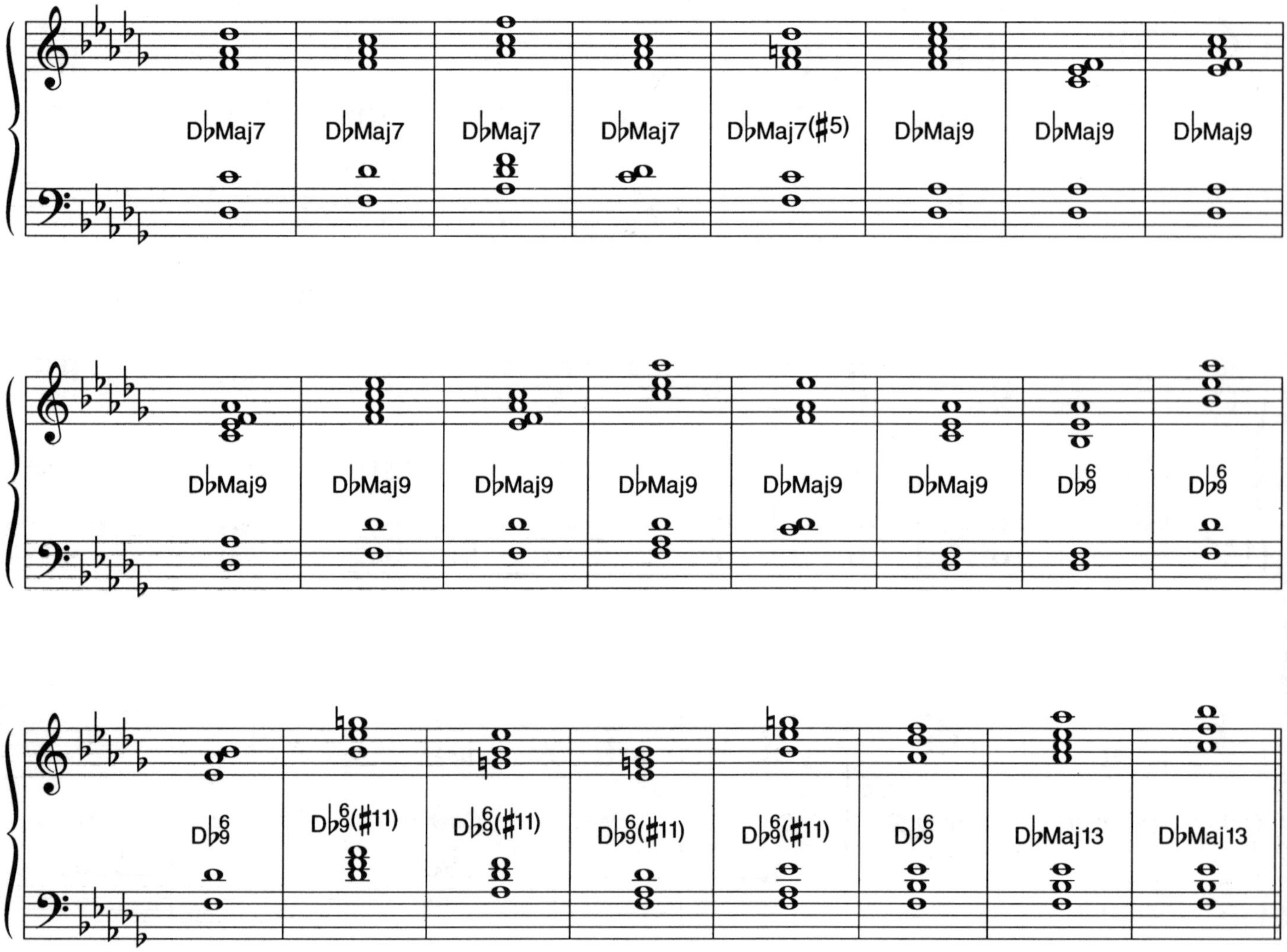

Minor Chords

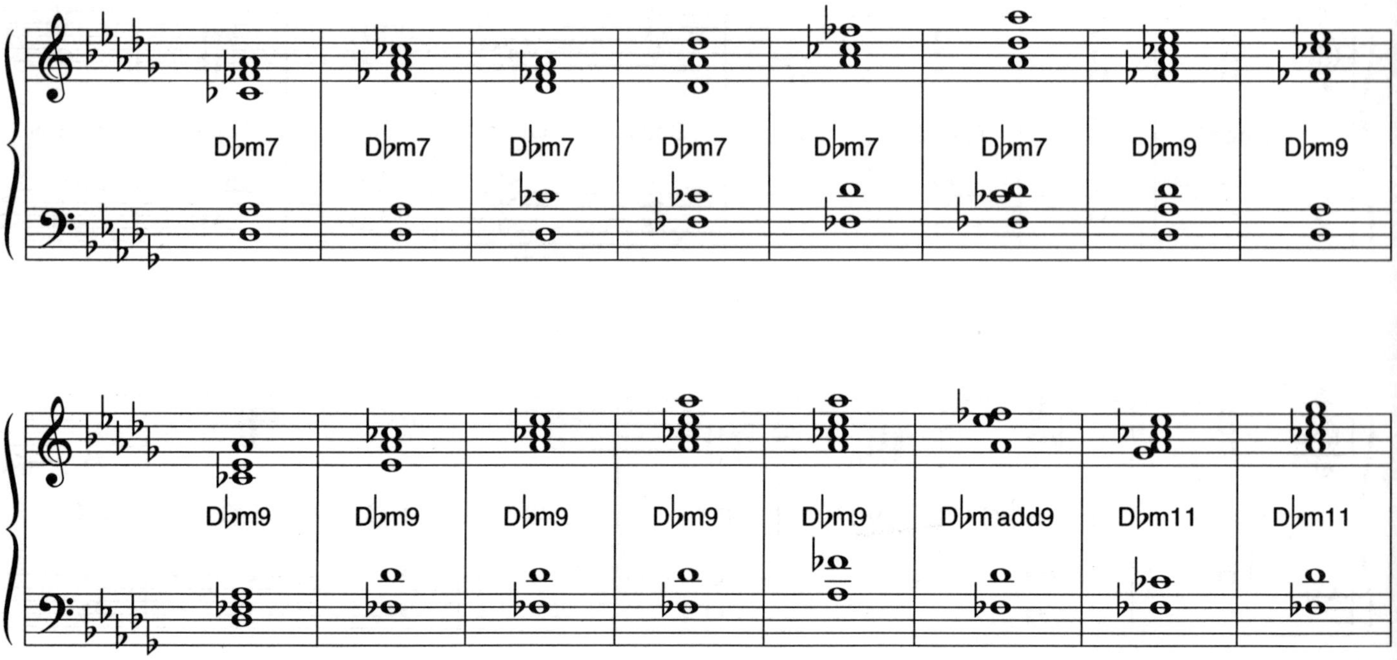

Chords-Key of D♭

Dbm11 Dbm11 Dbm11 Dbm11 Dbm6 Dbm6 Dbm6/9 Dbm6/9

Dominant Chords

Dbm6/9 Dbm(Maj7) Dbm9(Maj7) Dbm9(Maj7) Db7 Db7 Db7 Db7(#5)

Db7(#5) Db7(#5) Db7(b5) Db7(b5) Db9 Db9 Db9 Db7(b9)

Db7(b9) Db7(b9) Db7(b9) Db13(b9) Db7(#5 b9) Db7(b9) Db7(b5 b9) Db7(b5 b9)

Db7(b5 b9) Db7(b5 b9) Db7(#9) Db7(#5 #9) Db7(#9) Db7(#5 #9) Db7(#5 #9) Db11

35

Chords-Key of D♭

Db7(#9#5#11) Db7(#11) Db9(#11) Db13(#11) Db13sus Db13sus Db13 Db13

Diminished Chords

Db13 Db13 Db13 Db13 Db13(b9) Db13(#11) Dbm7(b5) Dbm7(b5)

Dbm7(b5) Dbm11(b5) Db°7 Db°Maj7 Dbm9(b5) Dbm11(b5) Dbm11(b5)

Suspended Chords

Dbadd9 Db6/9 Dbsus2 Dbsus Dbsus Dbsus2 Db9sus Db9sus Db9sus

Db9sus Db9sus(b5) Eb/Db Eb/Db Cb/Db Cb/Db Gb/Db Gb/Db

36

Chords-Key of D

Major Chords

Minor Chords

Chords-Key of D

| Dm11 | Dm11 | Dm11 | Dm11 | Dm6 | Dm6 | Dm$^6_9$ | Dm$^6_9$ |

Dominant Chords

| Dm$^6_9$ | Dm(Maj7) | Dm9(Maj7) | Dm9(Maj7) | D7 | D7 | D7 | D7(♯5) |

| D7(♯5) | D7(♯5) | D7(♭5) | D7(♭5) | D9 | D9 | D9 | D7(♭9) |

| D7(♭9) | D7(♭9) | D7(♭9) | D13(♭9) | D7($^{♯5}_{♭9}$) | D7(♭9) | D7($^{♭5}_{♭9}$) | D7($^{♭5}_{♭9}$) |

| D7($^{♭5}_{♭9}$) | D7($^{♭5}_{♭9}$) | D7(♯9) | D7($^{♯5}_{♯9}$) | D7(♯9) | D7($^{♯5}_{♯9}$) | D7($^{♯5}_{♯9}$) | D11 |

38

Chords-Key of D

| D7(#5#9#11) | D7(#11) | D9(#11) | D13(#11) | D13sus | D13sus | D13 | D13 |

Diminished Chords

| D13 | D13 | D13 | D13 | D13(♭9) | D13(#11) | Dm7(♭5) | Dm7(♭5) |

| Dm7(♭5) | Dm11(♭5) | D°7 | D°Maj7 | Dm9(♭5) | Dm11(♭5) | Dm11(♭5) |

Suspended Chords

| Dadd9 | D6/9 | Dsus2 | Dsus | Dsus | Dsus2 | D9sus | D9sus | D9sus |

| D9sus | D9sus(♭5) | E/D | E/D | C/D | C/D | G/D | G/D |

Chords-Key of E♭

Major Chords

Row 1: E♭Maj7 · E♭Maj7 · E♭Maj7 · E♭Maj7 · E♭Maj7(♯5) · E♭Maj9 · E♭Maj9 · E♭Maj9

Row 2: E♭Maj9 · E♭Maj9 · E♭Maj9 · E♭Maj9 · E♭Maj9 · E♭Maj9 · E♭⁶/₉ · E♭⁶/₉

Row 3: E♭⁶/₉ · E♭⁶/₉(♯11) · E♭⁶/₉(♯11) · E♭⁶/₉(♯11) · E♭⁶/₉(♯11) · E♭⁶/₉ · E♭Maj13 · E♭Maj13

Minor Chords

Row 4: E♭m7 · E♭m7 · E♭m7 · E♭m7 · E♭m7 · E♭m7 · E♭m9 · E♭m9

Row 5: E♭m9 · E♭m9 · E♭m9 · E♭m9 · E♭m9 · E♭m add9 · E♭m11 · E♭m11

Chords-Key of E♭

Ebm11 · Ebm11 · Ebm11 · Ebm11 · Ebm6 · Ebm6 · Ebm⁶/9 · Ebm⁶/9

Dominant Chords

Ebm⁶/9 · Ebm(Maj7) · Ebm9(Maj7) · Ebm9(Maj7) · Eb7 · Eb7 · Eb7 · Eb7(♯5)

Eb7(♯5) · Eb7(♯5) · Eb7(♭5) · Eb7(♭5) · Eb9 · Eb9 · Eb9 · Eb7(♭9)

Eb7(♭9) · Eb7(♭9) · Eb7(♭9) · Eb13(♭9) · Eb7(♯5/♭9) · Eb7(♭9) · Eb7(♭5/♭9) · Eb7(♭5/♭9)

Eb7(♭5/♭9) · Eb7(♭5/♭9) · Eb7(♯9) · Eb7(♯5/♯9) · Eb7(♯9) · Eb7(♯5/♯9) · Eb7(♯5/♯9) · Eb11

41

Chords-Key of E♭

Eb7(#5#9#11) Eb7(#11) Eb9(#11) Eb13(#11) Eb13sus Eb13sus Eb13 Eb13

Diminished Chords

Eb13 Eb13 Eb13 Eb13 Eb13(b9) Eb13(#11) Ebm7(b5) Ebm7(b5)

Ebm7(b5) Ebm11(b5) Eb°7 Eb°Maj7 Ebm9(b5) Ebm11(b5) Ebm11(b5)

Suspended Chords

Ebadd9 Eb6/9 Ebsus2 Ebsus Ebsus Ebsus2 Eb9sus Eb9sus Eb9sus

Eb9sus Eb9sus(b5) F/Eb F/Eb Db/Eb Db/Eb Ab/Eb Ab/Eb

Chords-Key of E

Major Chords

EMaj7	EMaj7	EMaj7	EMaj7	EMaj7($\sharp$5)	EMaj9	EMaj9	EMaj9

EMaj9	EMaj9	EMaj9	EMaj9	EMaj9	EMaj9	E$^6_9$	E$^6_9$

E$^6_9$	E$^{6}_{9}(\sharp 11)$	E$^{6}_{9}(\sharp 11)$	E$^{6}_{9}(\sharp 11)$	E$^{6}_{9}(\sharp 11)$	E$^6_9$	EMaj13	EMaj13

Minor Chords

Em7	Em7	Em7	Em7	Em7	Em7	Em9	Em9

Em9	Em9	Em9	Em9	Em9	Em add9	Em11	Em11

43

Chords-Key of E

Em11   Em11   Em11   Em11   Em6   Em6   Em$\frac{6}{9}$ Em$\frac{6}{9}$

Dominant Chords

Em$\frac{6}{9}$ Em(Maj7)   Em9(Maj7)   Em9(Maj7)   E7   E7   E7   E7(♯5)

E7(♯5)   E7(♯5)   E7(♭5)   E7(♭5)   E9   E9   E9   E7(♭9)

E7(♭9)   E7(♭9)   E7(♭9)   E13(♭9)   E7($^{\sharp5}_{\flat9}$)   E7(♭9)   E7($^{\flat5}_{\flat9}$)   E7($^{\flat5}_{\flat9}$)

E7($^{\flat5}_{\flat9}$)   E7($^{\flat5}_{\flat9}$)   E7(♯9)   E7($^{\sharp5}_{\sharp9}$)   E7(♯9)   E7($^{\sharp5}_{\sharp9}$)   E7($^{\sharp5}_{\sharp9}$)   E11

44

Chords-Key of E

E7($^{#5}_{#9#11}$)	E7(#11)	E9(#11)	E13(#11)	E13sus	E13sus	E13	E13

Diminished Chords

E13	E13	E13	E13	E13(b9)	E13(#11)	Em7(b5)	Em7(b5)

Em7(b5)	Em11(b5)	E°7	E°Maj7	Em9(b5)	Em11(b5)	Em11(b5)

Suspended Chords

Eadd9	E$^6_9$	Esus2	Esus	Esus	Esus2	E9sus	E9sus	E9sus

E9sus	E9sus(b5)	F#/E	F#/E	D/E	D/E	A/E	A/E

45

Chords-Key of F

Major Chords

FMaj7　FMaj7　FMaj7　FMaj7　FMaj7(♯5)　FMaj9　FMaj9　FMaj9

FMaj9　FMaj9　FMaj9　FMaj9　FMaj9　FMaj9　F$\frac{6}{9}$　F$\frac{6}{9}$

F$\frac{6}{9}$　F$\frac{6}{9}$(♯11)　F$\frac{6}{9}$(♯11)　F$\frac{6}{9}$(♯11)　F$\frac{6}{9}$(♯11)　F$\frac{6}{9}$　FMaj13　FMaj13

Minor Chords

Fm7　Fm7　Fm7　Fm7　Fm7　Fm7　Fm9　Fm9

Fm9　Fm9　Fm9　Fm9　Fm9　Fm add9　Fm11　Fm11

46

Chords-Key of F

Fm11   Fm11   Fm11   Fm11   Fm6   Fm6   Fm$\frac{6}{9}$ Fm$\frac{6}{9}$

Dominant Chords

Fm$\frac{6}{9}$ Fm(Maj7)   Fm9(Maj7)   Fm9(Maj7)   F7   F7   F7   F7($\sharp$5)

F7($\sharp$5)   F7($\sharp$5)   F7($\flat$5)   F7($\flat$5)   F9   F9   F9   F7($\flat$9)

F7($\flat$9)   F7($\flat$9)   F7($\flat$9)   F13($\flat$9)   F7$\left(\begin{smallmatrix}\sharp5\\\flat9\end{smallmatrix}\right)$ F7($\flat$9)   F7$\left(\begin{smallmatrix}\flat5\\\flat9\end{smallmatrix}\right)$ F7$\left(\begin{smallmatrix}\flat5\\\flat9\end{smallmatrix}\right)$

F7$\left(\begin{smallmatrix}\flat5\\\flat9\end{smallmatrix}\right)$ F7$\left(\begin{smallmatrix}\flat5\\\flat9\end{smallmatrix}\right)$ F7($\sharp$9)   F7$\left(\begin{smallmatrix}\sharp5\\\sharp9\end{smallmatrix}\right)$ F7($\sharp$9)   F7$\left(\begin{smallmatrix}\sharp5\\\sharp9\end{smallmatrix}\right)$ F7$\left(\begin{smallmatrix}\sharp5\\\sharp9\end{smallmatrix}\right)$ F11

Chords-Key of F

F7($\flat9\sharp5\sharp11$)　　F7($\sharp11$)　　F9($\sharp11$)　　F13($\sharp11$)　　F13sus　　F13sus　　F13　　F13

Diminished Chords

F13　　F13　　F13　　F13　　F13($\flat9$)　　F13($\sharp11$)　　Fm7($\flat5$)　　Fm7($\flat5$)

Fm7($\flat5$)　　Fm11($\flat5$)　　F°7　　F°Maj7　　Fm9($\flat5$)　　Fm11($\flat5$)　　Fm11($\flat5$)

Suspended Chords

Fadd9　　F$^6_9$　　Fsus2　　Fsus　　Fsus　　Fsus2　　F9sus　　F9sus　　F9sus

F9sus　　F9sus($\flat5$)　　G/F　　G/F　　E$\flat$/F　　E$\flat$/F　　B$\flat$/F　　B$\flat$/F

48

Chords-Key of F#

Minor Chords

49

Chords-Key of F♯

(First system chords, left to right)
F♯m11 | F♯m11 | F♯m11 | F♯m11 | F♯m6 | F♯m6 | F♯m⁶₉ | F♯m⁶₉

Dominant Chords

(Second system chords, left to right)
F♯m⁶₉ | F♯m(Maj7) | F♯m9(Maj7) | F♯m9(Maj7) | F♯7 | F♯7 | F♯7 | F♯7(♯5)

(Third system chords, left to right)
F♯7(♯5) | F♯7(♯5) | F♯7(♭5) | F♯7(♭5) | F♯9 | F♯9 | F♯9 | F♯7(♭9)

(Fourth system chords, left to right)
F♯7(♭9) | F♯7(♭9) | F♯7(♭9) | F♯13(♭9) | F♯7(♯5 ♭9) | F♯7(♭9) | F♯7(♭5 ♭9) | F♯7(♭5 ♭9)

(Fifth system chords, left to right)
F♯7(♭5 ♭9) | F♯7(♭5 ♭9) | F♯7(♯9) | F♯7(♯5 ♯9) | F♯7(♯9) | F♯7(♯5 ♯9) | F♯7(♯5 ♯9) | F♯11

Chords-Key of F#

Diminished Chords

Suspended Chords

Chords-Key of G

Major Chords

Minor Chords

Chords-Key of G

| Gm11 | Gm11 | Gm11 | Gm11 | Gm6 | Gm6 | Gm$^6_9$ | Gm$^6_9$ |

Dominant Chords

| Gm$^6_9$ | Gm(Maj7) | Gm9(Maj7) | Gm9(Maj7) | G7 | G7 | G7 | G7(♯5) |

| G7(♯5) | G7(♯5) | G7(♭5) | G7(♭5) | G9 | G9 | G9 | G7(♭9) |

| G7(♭9) | G7(♭9) | G7(♭9) | G13(♭9) | G7($^{♯5}_{♭9}$) | G7(♭9) | G7($^{♭5}_{♭9}$) | G7($^{♭5}_{♭9}$) |

| G7($^{♭5}_{♭9}$) | G7($^{♭5}_{♭9}$) | G7(♯9) | G7($^{♯5}_{♯9}$) | G7(♯9) | G7($^{♯5}_{♯9}$) | G7($^{♯5}_{♯9}$) | G11 |

Chords-Key of G

G7(#5#9#11) G7(#11) G9(#11) G13(#11) G13sus G13sus G13 G13

Diminished Chords

G13 G13 G13 G13 G13(b9) G13(#11) Gm7(b5) Gm7(b5)

Gm7(b5) Gm11(b5) G°7 G°Maj7 Gm9(b5) Gm11(b5) Gm11(b5)

Suspended Chords

Gadd9 G6/9 Gsus2 Gsus Gsus Gsus2 G9sus G9sus G9sus

G9sus G9sus(b5) A/G A/G F/G F/G C/G C/G

Chords-Key of A♭

Chords-Key of A♭

Abm11 Abm11 Abm11 Abm11 Abm6 Abm6 Abm⁶₉ Abm⁶₉

Dominant Chords

Abm⁶₉ Abm(Maj7) Abm9(Maj7) Abm9(Maj7) Ab7 Ab7 Ab7 Ab7(♯5)

Ab7(♯5) Ab7(♯5) Ab7(♭5) Ab7(♭5) Ab9 Ab9 Ab9 Ab7(♭9)

Ab7(♭9) Ab7(♭9) Ab7(♭9) Ab13(♭9) Ab7(♯5♭9) Ab7(♭9) Ab7(♭5♭9) Ab7(♭5♭9)

Ab7(♭5♭9) Ab7(♭5♭9) Ab7(♯9) Ab7(♯5♯9) Ab7(♯9) Ab7(♯5♯9) Ab7(♯5♯9) Ab11

Chords-Key of A♭

Row 1: A♭7(♯9♯11) | A♭7(♯11) | A♭9(♯11) | A♭13(♯11) | A♭13sus | A♭13sus | A♭13 | A♭13

Diminished Chords

Row 2: A♭13 | A♭13 | A♭13 | A♭13 | A♭13(♭9) | A♭13(♯11) | A♭m7(♭5) | A♭m7(♭5)

Row 3: A♭m7(♭5) | A♭m11(♭5) | A♭°7 | A♭°Maj7 | A♭m9(♭5) | A♭m11(♭5) | A♭m11(♭5)

Suspended Chords

Row 4: A♭add9 | A♭⁶/₉ | A♭sus2 | A♭sus | A♭sus | A♭sus2 | A♭9sus | A♭9sus | A♭9sus

Row 5: A♭9sus | A♭9sus(♭5) | B♭/A♭ | B♭/A♭ | G♭/A♭ | G♭/A♭ | D♭/A♭ | D♭/A♭

57

Chords-Key of A

Major Chords

| AMaj7 | AMaj7 | AMaj7 | AMaj7 | AMaj7(#5) | AMaj9 | AMaj9 | AMaj9 |

| AMaj9 | AMaj9 | AMaj9 | AMaj9 | AMaj9 | AMaj9 | A$_9^6$ | A$_9^6$ |

| A$_9^6$ | A$_9^{6(\#11)}$ | A$_9^{6(\#11)}$ | A$_9^{6(\#11)}$ | A$_9^{6(\#11)}$ | A$_9^6$ | AMaj13 | AMaj13 |

Minor Chords

| Am7 | Am7 | Am7 | Am7 | Am7 | Am7 | Am9 | Am9 |

| Am9 | Am9 | Am9 | Am9 | Am9 | Am add9 | Am11 | Am11 |

58

Chords-Key of A

| Am11 | Am11 | Am11 | Am11 | Am6 | Am6 | Am$^6_9$ | Am$^6_9$ |

Dominant Chords

| Am$^6_9$ | Am(Maj7) | Am9(Maj7) | Am9(Maj7) | A7 | A7 | A7 | A7(♯5) |

| A7(♯5) | A7(♯5) | A7(♭5) | A7(♭5) | A9 | A9 | A9 | A7(♭9) |

| A7(♭9) | A7(♭9) | A7(♭9) | A13(♭9) | A7($^{♯5}_{♭9}$) | A7(♭9) | A7($^{♭5}_{♭9}$) | A7($^{♭5}_{♭9}$) |

| A7($^{♭5}_{♭9}$) | A7($^{♭5}_{♭9}$) | A7(♯9) | A7($^{♯5}_{♯9}$) | A7(♯9) | A7($^{♯5}_{♯9}$) | A7($^{♯5}_{♯9}$) | A11 |

59

Chords-Key of A

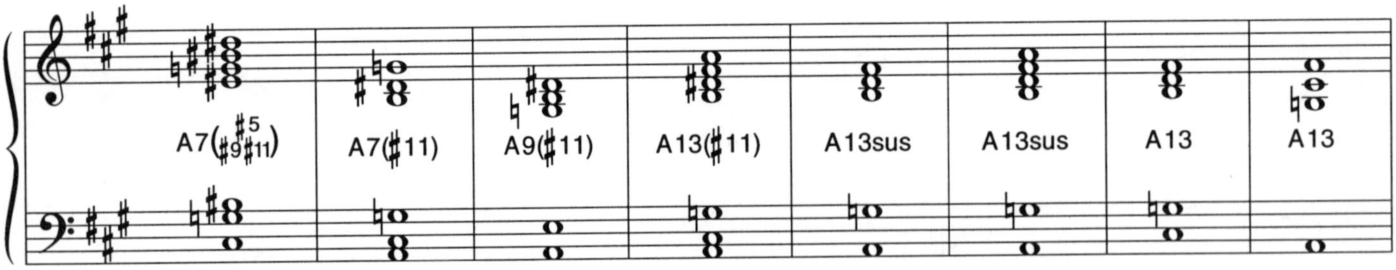

Chords (top row): A7($\sharp 5$/$\sharp 9$/$\sharp 11$) A7($\sharp 11$) A9($\sharp 11$) A13($\sharp 11$) A13sus A13sus A13 A13

Diminished Chords

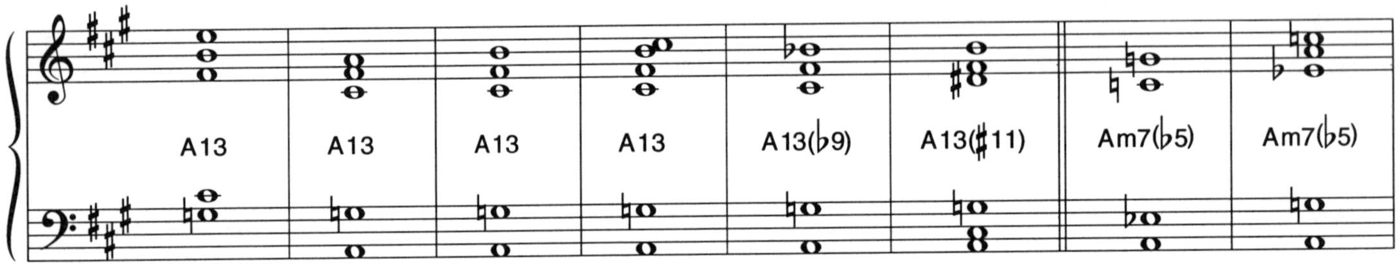

Chords (second row): A13 A13 A13 A13 A13($\flat 9$) A13($\sharp 11$) Am7($\flat 5$) Am7($\flat 5$)

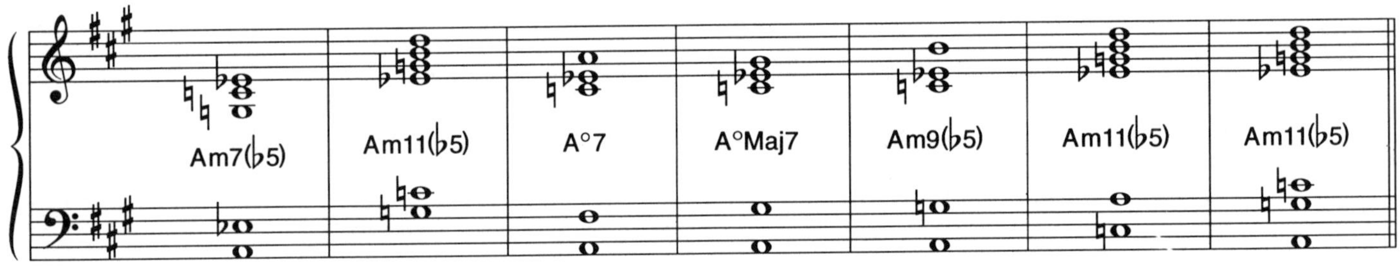

Chords (third row): Am7($\flat 5$) Am11($\flat 5$) A°7 A°Maj7 Am9($\flat 5$) Am11($\flat 5$) Am11($\flat 5$)

Suspended Chords

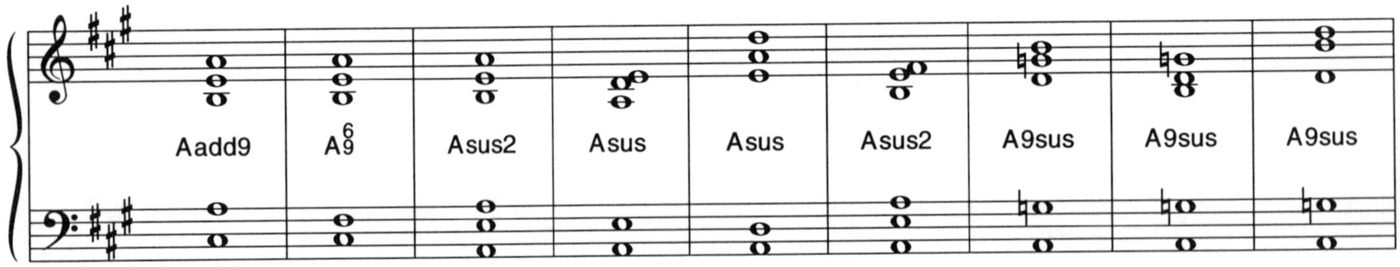

Chords (fourth row): Aadd9 A$^6_9$ Asus2 Asus Asus Asus2 A9sus A9sus A9sus

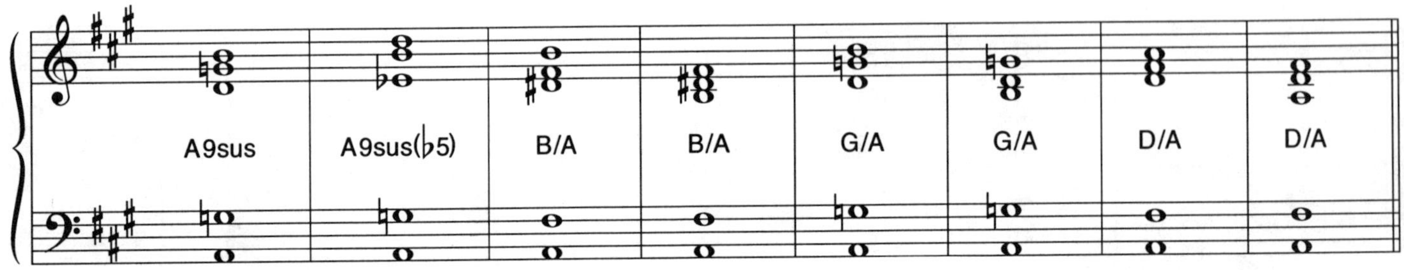

Chords (fifth row): A9sus A9sus($\flat 5$) B/A B/A G/A G/A D/A D/A

Chords-Key of B♭

Major Chords

| B♭Maj7 | B♭Maj7 | B♭Maj7 | B♭Maj7 | B♭Maj7(♯5) | B♭Maj9 | B♭Maj9 | B♭Maj9 |

| B♭Maj9 | B♭Maj9 | B♭Maj9 | B♭Maj9 | B♭Maj9 | B♭Maj9 | B♭9/6 | B♭9/6 |

| B♭9/6 | B♭9/6(♯11) | B♭9/6(♯11) | B♭9/6(♯11) | B♭9/6(♯11) | B♭9/6 | B♭Maj13 | B♭Maj13 |

Minor Chords

| B♭m7 | B♭m7 | B♭m7 | B♭m7 | B♭m7 | B♭m7 | B♭m9 | B♭m9 |

| B♭m9 | B♭m9 | B♭m9 | B♭m9 | B♭m9 | B♭m add9 | B♭m11 | B♭m11 |

61

Chords-Key of B♭

Bbm11 · Bbm11 · Bbm11 · Bbm11 · Bbm6 · Bbm6 · Bbm9⁶ · Bbm9⁶

Dominant Chords

Bbm9⁶ · Bbm(Maj7) · Bbm9(Maj7) · Bbm9(Maj7) · Bb7 · Bb7 · Bb7 · Bb7(♯5)

Bb7(♯5) · Bb7(♯5) · Bb7(♭5) · Bb7(♭5) · Bb9 · Bb9 · Bb9 · Bb7(♭9)

Bb7(♭9) · Bb7(♭9) · Bb7(♭9) · Bb13(♭9) · Bb7(♯5♭9) · Bb7(♭9) · Bb7(♭5♭9) · Bb7(♭5♭9)

Bb7(♭5♭9) · Bb7(♭5♭9) · Bb7(♯9) · Bb7(♯5♯9) · Bb7(♯9) · Bb7(♯5♯9) · Bb7(♯5♯9) · Bb11

Chords-Key of B♭

Bb7(#9#5#11)   Bb7(#11)   Bb9(#11)   Bb13(#11)   Bb13sus   Bb13sus   Bb13   Bb13

Diminished Chords

Bb13   Bb13   Bb13   Bb13   Bb13(b9)   Bb13(#11)   Bbm7(b5)   Bbm7(b5)

Bbm7(b5)   Bbm11(b5)   Bb°7   Bb°Maj7   Bbm9(b5)   Bbm11(b5)   Bbm11(b5)

Suspended Chords

Bbadd9   Bb6/9   Bbsus2   Bbsus   Bbsus   Bbsus2   Bb9sus   Bb9sus   Bb9sus

Bb9sus   Bb9sus(b5)   C/Bb   C/Bb   Ab/Bb   Ab/Bb   Eb/Bb   Eb/Bb

Chords-Key of B

Major Chords

| BMaj7 | BMaj7 | BMaj7 | BMaj7 | BMaj7(#5) | BMaj9 | BMaj9 | BMaj9 |

| BMaj9 | BMaj9 | BMaj9 | BMaj9 | BMaj9 | BMaj9 | B$\frac{6}{9}$ | B$\frac{6}{9}$ |

| B$\frac{6}{9}$ | B$\frac{6}{9}$(#11) | B$\frac{6}{9}$(#11) | B$\frac{6}{9}$(#11) | B$\frac{6}{9}$(#11) | B$\frac{6}{9}$ | BMaj13 | BMaj13 |

Minor Chords

| Bm7 | Bm7 | Bm7 | Bm7 | Bm7 | Bm7 | Bm9 | Bm9 |

| Bm9 | Bm9 | Bm9 | Bm9 | Bm9 | Bm add9 | Bm11 | Bm11 |

Chords-Key of B

| Bm11 | Bm11 | Bm11 | Bm11 | Bm6 | Bm6 | Bm⁶/9 | Bm⁶/9 |

Dominant Chords

| Bm⁶/9 | Bm(Maj7) | Bm9(Maj7) | Bm9(Maj7) | B7 | B7 | B7 | B7(♯5) |

| B7(♯5) | B7(♯5) | B7(♭5) | B7(♭5) | B9 | B9 | B9 | B7(♭9) |

| B7(♭9) | B7(♭9) | B7(♭9) | B13(♭9) | B7(♯5/♭9) | B7(♭9) | B7(♭5/♭9) | B7(♭5/♭9) |

| B7(♭5/♭9) | B7(♭5/♭9) | B7(♯9) | B7(♯5/♭9) | B7(♯9) | B7(♯5/♯9) | B7(♯5/♯9) | B11 |

65

Chords-Key of B

B7(#9#11#5) B7(#11) B9(#11) B13(#11) B13sus B13sus B13 B13

Diminished Chords

B13 B13 B13 B13 B13(♭9) B13(#11) Bm7(♭5) Bm7(♭5)

Bm7(♭5) Bm11(♭5) B°7 B°Maj7 Bm9(♭5) Bm11(♭5) Bm11(♭5)

Suspended Chords

Badd9 B⁶₉ Bsus2 Bsus Bsus Bsus2 B9sus B9sus B9sus

B9sus B9sus(♭5) C#/B C#/B A/B A/B E/B E/B

Chords-Harmonizing C or B♯

Major Chords

CMaj7 | CMaj7(♯5) | D♭Maj7 | D♭Maj9 | D♭Maj9 | D♭Maj7 | E♭9/6 | E♭9/6(♯11)

E♭Maj13 | FMaj9 | FMaj9 | F9/6 | FMaj9 | FMaj13 | F9/6 | G♭9/6(♯11)

G♭9/6(♯11) | A♭Maj7 | A♭Maj9 | A♭9/6 | B♭Maj9 | B♭9/6(♯11) | B♭Maj9 | B♭Maj9

Minor Chords

Cm6 | Cm7 | Cm9/6 | Cm(Maj7) | Dm9 | Dm7 | E♭m6 | Fm7

Fm7 | Fm9 | Fm7 | Fm9 | Fm11 | Fm9/6 | Fm9 | F9sus

67

Chords-Harmonizing C or B♯

| Fm9(Maj7) | Gm11 | Am7 | Am9 | B♭m9 | B♭m11 | B♭m⁶₉ | B♭m9 |

Dominant Chords

| B♭m11 | B♭m9(Maj7) | B♭m9 | C7 | C7(♯5) | C7(♯5) | C13(♯11) | C7(♭5) |

| C13 | C13sus | C7(♭9) | C7(♭9) | C7(♯5♯9) | D7 | D7(♭5) | D9 |

| D9 | D7(♭9) | D7(♯11) | E♭13(♭9) | E♭13sus | E♭13 | E♭13 | E7(♯5♯9) |

| E7(♯5) | F7 | F9 | F7(♭9) | F13 | F7(♯9) | G♭7(♯5♯9♯11) | G♭7(♯11) |

Chords-Harmonizing C or B♯

G9sus | A♭13 | A7(♯9) | A7($^{♯5}_{♯9}$) | B♭9sus | B♭13 | B♭13(♯11) | B♭11

Diminished Chords

B7(♭9) | B7($^{♯5}_{♭9}$) | B7($^{♭5}_{♭9}$) | B7($^{♭5}_{♭9}$) | B13(♭9) | C°7 | D♭°Maj7 | Dm7(♭5)

F♯m7(♭5) | G9sus(♭5) | Gm11(♭5) | Gm11(♭5) | Gm11(♭5) | Am7(♭5) | B♭m9(♭5) | B7($^{♭5}_{♭9}$)

Suspended Chords

B7($^{♭5}_{♭9}$) | C$^6_9$ | Cadd9 | Csus2 | D9sus | E♭6sus2 | Fm11 | Fsus

Gsus | B♭9sus | C/D | C/B♭ | F/C | F/E♭ | A♭/B♭ | A♭/E♭

69

Chords-Harmonizing D♭ or C♯

Major Chords

DbMaj7 | DbMaj7(#5) | DMaj7 | DMaj9 | DMaj9 | DMaj7 | E⁶/₉ | E⁶/₉(#11)

EMaj13 | F#Maj9 | F#Maj9 | F#⁶/₉ | F#Maj9 | F#Maj13 | F#⁶/₉ | G⁶/₉(#11)

G⁶/₉(#11) | AMaj7 | AMaj9 | A⁶/₉ | BMaj9 | B⁶/₉(#11) | BMaj9 | BMaj9

Minor Chords

Dbm6 | Dbm7 | Dbm⁶/₉ | Dbm(Maj7) | Ebm9 | Ebm7 | Em6 | F#m7

F#m7 | F#m9 | F#m7 | F#m9 | F#m11 | F#m⁶/₉ | F#m9 | F#9sus

Chords-Harmonizing D♭ or C♯

F♯m9(Maj7) A♭m11 B♭m7 B♭m9 Bm9 Bm11 Bm$^6_9$ Bm9

Dominant Chords

Bm11 Bm9(Maj7) Bm9 D♭7 D♭7(♯5) D♭7(♯5) D♭13(♯11) D♭7(♭5)

D♭13 D♭13sus D♭7(♭9) D♭7(♭9) D♭7($^{♯5}_{♭9}$) E♭7 E♭7(♭5) E♭9

E♭9 E♭7(♭9) E♭7(♯11) E13(♭9) E13sus E13 E13 F7($^{♯5}_{♯9}$)

F7(♯5) F♯7 F♯9 F♯7(♭9) F♯13 F♯7(♯9) G7($^{♯5}_{♯9♯11}$) G7(♯11)

71

Chords-Harmonizing D♭ or C♯

Ab9sus | A13 | Bb7(♯9) | Bb7(♯5 ♭9) | B9sus | B13 | B13(♯11) | B11

Diminished Chords

C7(♭9) | C7(♯5 ♭9) | C7(♭5 ♭9) | C7(♭5 ♭9) | C13(♭9) | Db°7 | D°Maj7 | Ebm7(♭5)

Gm7(♭5) | Ab9sus(♭5) | Abm11(♭5) | Abm11(♭5) | Abm11(♭5) | Bbm7(♭5) | Bm9(♭5) | C7(♭5 ♭9)

Suspended Chords

C7(♭5 ♭9) | Db6/9 | Dbadd9 | Dbsus2 | Eb9sus | E6sus2 | F♯m11 | F♯sus

Absus | B9sus | Db/Eb | Db/Cb | F♯/C♯ | F♯/E | A/B | A/E

72

Chords-Harmonizing D

Major Chords

DMaj7	DMaj7(#5)	E♭Maj7	E♭Maj9	E♭Maj9	E♭Maj7	F$^6_9$	F$^6_9$(#11)

FMaj13	GMaj9	GMaj9	G$^6_9$	GMaj9	GMaj13	G$^6_9$	A♭$^6_9$(#11)

A♭$^6_9$(#11)	B♭Maj7	B♭Maj9	B♭$^6_9$	CMaj9	C$^6_9$(#11)	CMaj9	CMaj9

Minor Chords

Dm6	Dm7	Dm$^6_9$	Dm(Maj7)	Em9	Em7	Fm6	Gm7

Gm7	Gm9	Gm7	Gm9	Gm11	Gm$^6_9$	Gm9	G9sus

Chords-Harmonizing D

Gm9(Maj7) Am11 Bm7 Bm9 Cm9 Cm11 Cm$^6_9$ Cm9

Dominant Chords

Cm11 Cm9(Maj7) Cm9 D7 D7($\sharp$5) D7($\sharp$5) D13($\sharp$11) D7($\flat$5)

D13 D13sus D7($\flat$9) D7($\flat$9) D7($^{\sharp5}_{\sharp9}$) E7 E7($\flat$5) E9

E9 E7($\flat$9) E7($\sharp$11) F13($\flat$9) F13sus F13 F13 G$\flat$7($^{\sharp5}_{\sharp9}$)

G$\flat$7($\sharp$5) G7 G9 G7($\flat$9) G13 G7($\sharp$9) A$\flat$7($^{\sharp5}_{\sharp9\sharp11}$) A$\flat$7($\sharp$11)

Chords-Harmonizing D

A9sus   Bb13   B7(#9)   Cb7($^{#5}_{b9}$)   C9sus   C13   C13(#11)   C11

Diminished Chords

C#7(b9)   C#7($^{#5}_{b9}$)   C#7($^{b5}_{b9}$)   C#7($^{b5}_{b9}$)   C#13(b9)   D°7   Eb°Maj7   Em7(b5)

G#m7(b5)   A9sus(b5)   Am11(b5)   Am11(b5)   Am11(b5)   Bm7(b5)   Cm9(b5)   C#7($^{b5}_{b9}$)

Suspended Chords

C#7($^{b5}_{b9}$)   D$^6_9$ Dadd9   Dsus2   E9sus   F6sus2   Gm11   Gsus

Asus   C9sus   D/E   D/C   G/D   G/F   Bb/C   Bb/F

Chords-Harmonizing E♭ or D♯

Major Chords

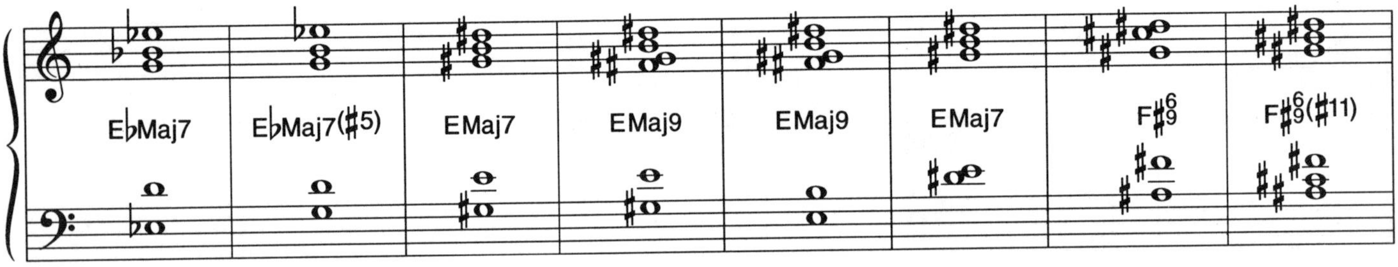

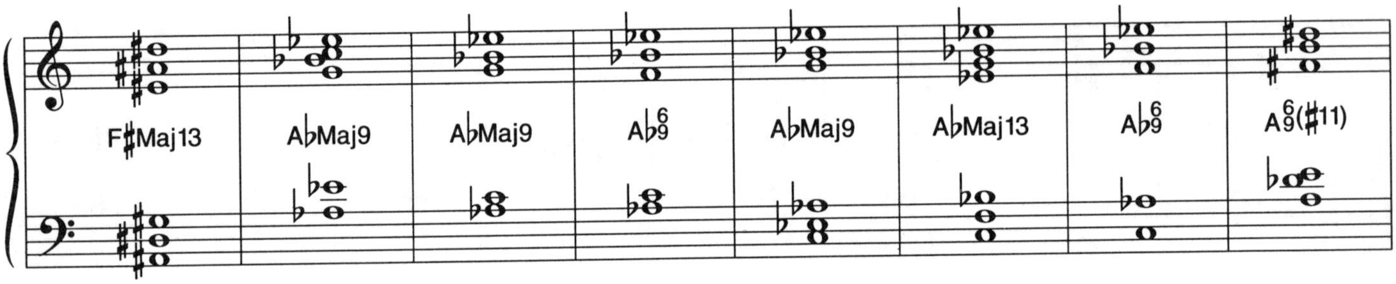

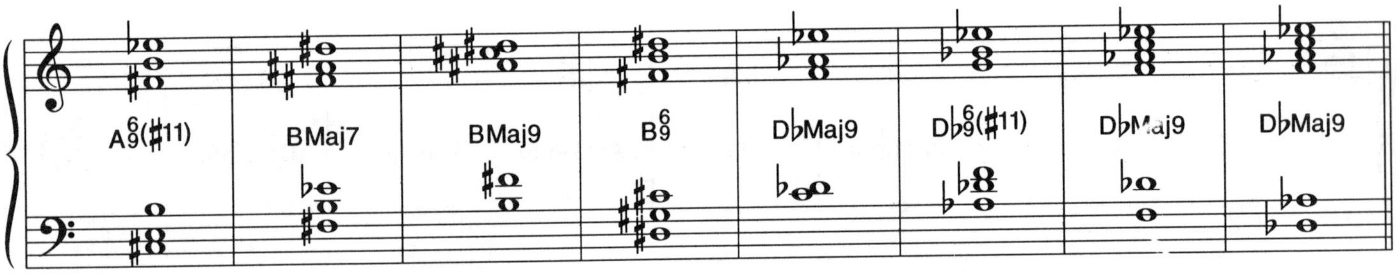

Minor Chords

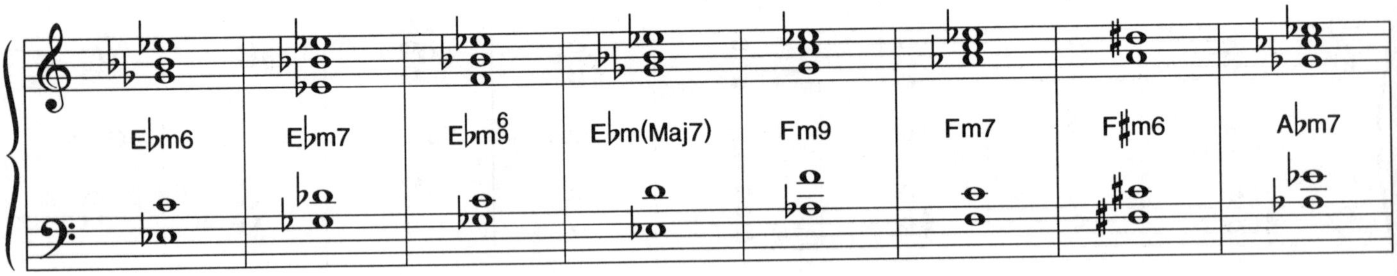

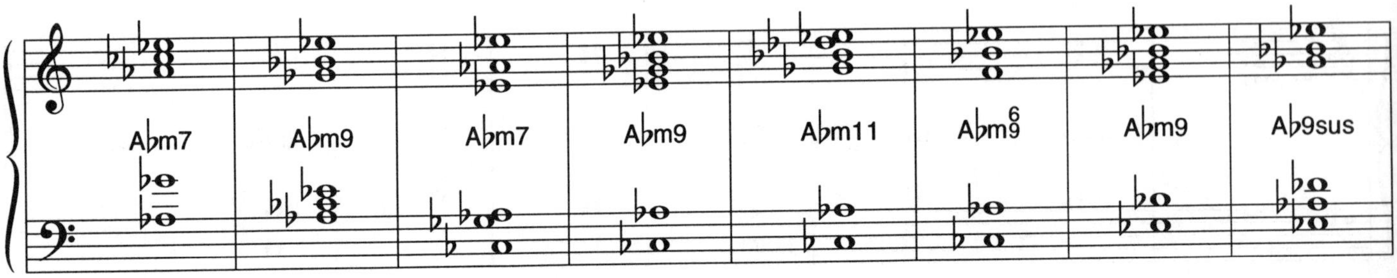

Chords-Harmonizing E♭ or D♯

Abm9(Maj7)   B♭m11   Cm7   Cm9   D♭m9   D♭m11   D♭m⁶/9   D♭m9

Dominant Chords

D♭m11   D♭m9(Maj7)   D♭m9   E♭7   E♭7(♯5)   E♭7(♯5)   E♭13(♯11)   E♭7(♭5)

E♭13   E♭13sus   E♭7(♭9)   E♭7(♭9)   E♭7(♯5/♭9)   F7   F7(♭5)   F9

F9   F7(♭9)   F7(♯11)   F♯13(♭9)   F♯13sus   F♯13   F♯13   G7(♯5/♭9)

G7(♯5)   A♭7   A♭9   A♭7(♭9)   A♭13   A♭7(♯9)   A7(♯5/♯9♯11)   A7(♯11)

77

Chords-Harmonizing E♭ or D♯

Row 1: Bb9sus | B13 | C7(♯9) | C7(♯5♭9) | Db9sus | Db13 | Db13(♯11) | Db11

Diminished Chords

Row 2: D7(♭9) | D7(♯5♭9) | D7(♭5♭9) | D7(♭5♭9) | D13(♭9) | Eb°7 | E°Maj7 | Fm7(♭5)

Row 3: Am7(♭5) | Bb9sus(♭5) | Bbm11(♭5) | Bbm11(♭5) | Bbm11(♭5) | Cm7(♭5) | Dbm9(♭5) | D7(♭5♭9)

Suspended Chords

Row 4: D7(♭5♭9) | Eb6/9 | Ebadd9 | Ebsus2 | F9sus | F♯6sus2 | Abm11 | Absus

Row 5: Bbsus | Db9sus | Eb/F | Eb/Db | Ab/Eb | Ab/F♯ | B/Db | B/F♯

Chords-Harmonizing E or F♭

Major Chords

EMaj7	EMaj7(♯5)	FMaj7	FMaj9	FMaj9	FMaj7	G⁶/₉	G⁶/₉(♯11)

GMaj13	AMaj9	AMaj9	A⁶/₉	AMaj9	AMaj13	A⁶/₉	B♭⁶/₉(♯11)

B♭⁶/₉(♯11)	CMaj7	CMaj9	C⁶/₉	DMaj9	D⁶/₉(♯11)	DMaj9	DMaj9

Minor Chords

Em6	Em7	Em⁶/₉	Em(Maj7)	F♯m9	F♯m7	Gm6	Am7

Am7	Am9	Am7	Am9	Am11	Am⁶/₉	Am9	A9sus

79

Chords-Harmonizing E or F♭

Am9(Maj7) Bm11 C#m7 C#m9 Dm9 Dm11 Dm⁶/9 Dm9

Dominant Chords

Dm11 Dm9(Maj7) Dm9 E7 E7(#5) E7(#5) E13(#11) E7(♭5)

E13 E13sus E7(♭9) E7(♭9) E7(#5/♭9) F#7 F#7(♭5) F#9

F#9 F#7(♭9) F#7(#11) G13(♭9) G13sus G13 G13 A♭7(#5/♭9)

A♭7(#5) A7 A9 A7(♭9) A13 A7(#9) B♭7(#5/#9 #11) B♭7(#11)

Chords-Harmonizing E or F♭

B9sus C13 D♭7(♯9) D♭7($^{♯5}_{♭9}$) D9sus D13 D13(♯11) D11

Diminished Chords

E♭7(♭9) E♭7($^{♯5}_{♭9}$) E♭7($^{♭5}_{♭9}$) E♭7($^{♭5}_{♭9}$) E♭13(♭9) E°7 F°Maj7 F♯m7(♭5)

B♭m7(♭5) B9sus(♭5) Bm11(♭5) Bm11(♭5) Bm11(♭5) D♭m7(♭5) Dm9(♭5) E♭7($^{♭5}_{♭9}$)

Suspended Chords

E♭7($^{♭5}_{♭9}$) E$^6_9$ Eadd9 Esus2 F♯9sus G6sus2 Am11 Asus

Bsus D9sus E/F♯ E/D A/E A/G C/D C/G

Chords-Harmonizing F or E♯

Row 1: FMaj7 | FMaj7(♯5) | F♯Maj7 | F♯Maj9 | F♯Maj9 | F♯Maj7 | A♭⁶/9 | A♭⁶/9(♯11)

Row 2: A♭Maj13 | B♭Maj9 | B♭Maj9 | B♭⁶/9 | B♭Maj9 | B♭Maj13 | B♭⁶/9 | B⁶/9(♯11)

Row 3: B⁶/9(♯11) | D♭Maj7 | D♭Maj9 | D♭⁶/9 | E♭Maj9 | E♭⁶/9(♯11) | E♭Maj9 | E♭Maj9

Minor Chords

Row 4: Fm6 | Fm7 | Fm⁶/9 | Fm(Maj7) | Gm9 | Gm7 | A♭m6 | B♭m7

Row 5: B♭m7 | B♭m9 | B♭m7 | B♭m9 | B♭m11 | B♭m⁶/9 | B♭m9 | B♭9sus

Chords-Harmonizing F or E♯

| B♭m9(Maj7) | Cm11 | Dm7 | Dm9 | E♭m9 | E♭m11 | E♭m⁶9 | E♭m9 |

Dominant Chords

| E♭m11 | E♭m9(Maj7) | E♭m9 | F7 | F7(♯5) | F7(♯5) | F13(♯11) | F7(♭5) |

| F13 | F13sus | F7(♭9) | F7(♭9) | F7(♯5♯9) | G7 | G7(♭5) | G9 |

| G9 | G7(♭9) | G7(♯11) | A♭13(♭9) | A♭13sus | A♭13 | A♭13 | A7(♯5♯9) |

| A7(♯5) | B♭7 | B♭9 | B♭7(♭9) | B♭13 | B♭7(♯9) | B7(♯5♯9♯11) | B7(♯11) |

Chords-Harmonizing F or E♯

C9sus   D♭13   D7(♯9)   D7($^{♯5}_{♭9}$)   E♭9sus   E♭13   E♭13(♯11)   E♭11

Diminished Chords

E7(♭9)   E7($^{♯5}_{♭9}$)   E7($^{♭5}_{♭9}$)   E7($^{♭5}_{♭9}$)   E13(♭9)   F°7   F♯°Maj7   Gm7(♭5)

Bm7(♭5)   C9sus(♭5)   Cm11(♭5)   Cm11(♭5)   Cm11(♭5)   Dm7(♭5)   E♭m9(♭5)   E7($^{♭5}_{♭9}$)

Suspended Chords

E7($^{♭5}_{♭9}$)   F$^6_9$ Fadd9   Fsus2   G9sus   A♭6sus2   B♭m11   B♭sus

Csus   E♭9sus   F/G   F/E♭   B♭/F   B♭/A♭   D♭/E♭   D♭/A♭

Major Chords

F♯Maj7	F♯Maj7(♯5)	GMaj7	GMaj9	GMaj9	GMaj7	A$_9^6$	A$_9^6$(♯11)

AMaj13	BMaj9	BMaj9	B$_9^6$	BMaj9	BMaj13	B$_9^6$	C$_9^6$(♯11)

C$_9^6$(♯11)	DMaj7	DMaj9	D$_9^6$	EMaj9	E$_9^6$(♯11)	EMaj9	EMaj9

Minor Chords

F♯m6	F♯m7	F♯m$_9^6$	F♯m(Maj7)	A♭m9	A♭m7	Am6	Bm7

Bm7	Bm9	Bm7	Bm9	Bm11	Bm$_9^6$	Bm9	B9sus

Chords-Harmonizing F♯ or G♭

Bm9(Maj7)	D♭m11	E♭m7	E♭m9	Em9	Em11	Em6/9	Em9

Dominant Chords

Em11	Em9(Maj7)	Em9	F♯7	F♯7(♯5)	F♯7(♯5)	F♯13(♯11)	F♯7(♭5)

F♯13	F♯13sus	F♯7(♭9)	F♯7(♭9)	F♯7(♯5/♭9)	A♭7	A♭7(♭5)	A♭9

A♭9	A♭7(♭9)	A♭7(♯11)	A13(♭9)	A13sus	A13	A13	B♭7(♯5/♯9)

B♭7(♯5)	B7	B9	B7(♭9)	B13	B7(♯9)	C7(♯5/♯9/♯11)	C7(♯11)

Chords-Harmonizing F♯ or G♭

Db9sus	D13	Eb7(#9)	Eb7(#5 b9)	E9sus	E13	E13(#11)	E11

Diminished Chords

F7(b9)	F7(#5 b9)	F7(b5 b9)	F7(b5 b9)	F13(b9)	F#°7	G°Maj7	Abm7(b5)

Cm7(b5)	Db9sus(b5)	Dbm11(b5)	Dbm11(b5)	Dbm11(b5)	Ebm7(b5)	Em9(b5)	F7(b5 b9)

Suspended Chords

F7(b5 b9)	F#6 #9	F#add9	F#sus2	Ab9sus	A6sus2	Bm11	Bsus

Dbsus	E9sus	F#/Ab	F#/E	B/F#	B/A	D/E	D/A

Chords-Harmonizing G

Major Chords

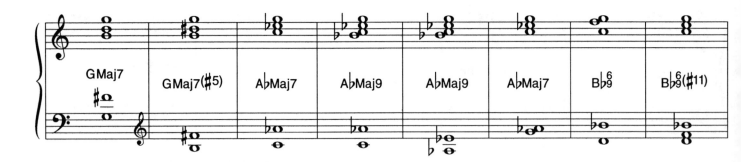

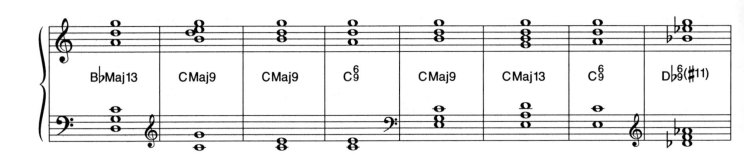

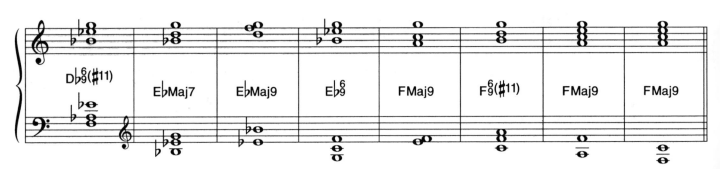

Minor Chords

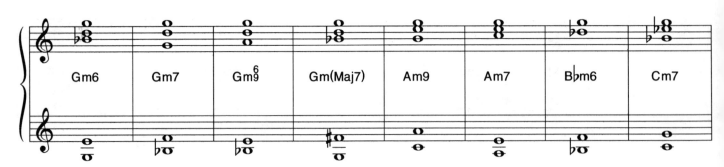

Chords-Harmonizing G

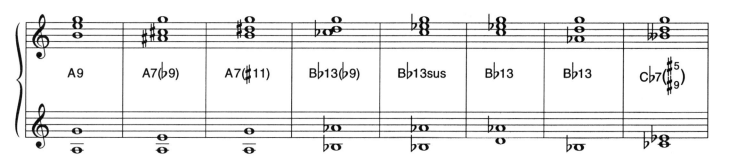

| Cm9(Maj7) | Dm11 | Em7 | Em9 | Fm9 | Fm11 | Fm⁶⁄₉ | Fm9 |

Dominant Chords

| Fm11 | Fm9(Maj7) | Fm9 | G7 | G7(♯5) | G7(♯5) | G13(♯11) | G7(♭5) |

| G13 | G13sus | G7(♭9) | G7(♭9) | G7(♯5♯9) | A7 | A7(♭5) | A9 |

| A9 | A7(♭9) | A7(♯11) | B♭13(♭9) | B♭13sus | B♭13 | B♭13 | C♭7(♯5♯9) |

| C♭7(♯5) | C7 | C9 | C7(♭9) | C13 | C7(♯9) | D♭7(♯5♯9♯11) | D♭7(♯11) |

Chords-Harmonizing G

D9sus Eb13 E7(#9) E7($^{#5}_{b9}$) F9sus F13 F13(#11) F11

Diminished Chords

F#7(b9) F#7($^{#5}_{b9}$) F#7($^{b5}_{b9}$) F#7($^{b5}_{b9}$) F#13(b9) G°7 Ab°Maj7 Am7(b5)

Dbm7(b5) D9sus(b5) Dm11(b5) Dm11(b5) Dm11(b5) Em7(b5) Fm9(b5) F#7($^{b5}_{b9}$)

Suspended Chords

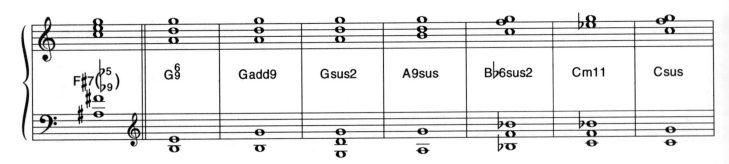

F#7($^{b5}_{b9}$) G$^{6}_{9}$ Gadd9 Gsus2 A9sus Bb6sus2 Cm11 Csus

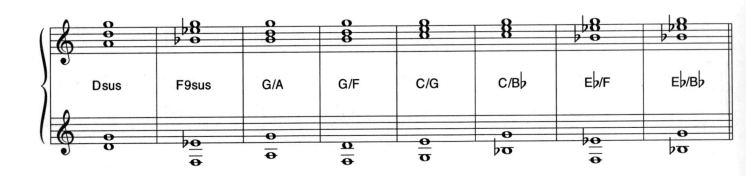

Dsus F9sus G/A G/F C/G C/Bb Eb/F Eb/Bb

Major Chords

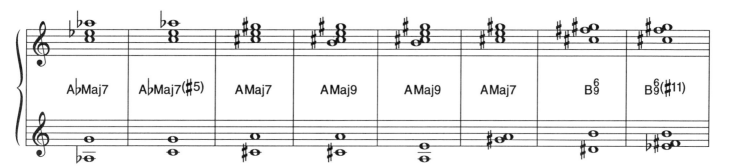

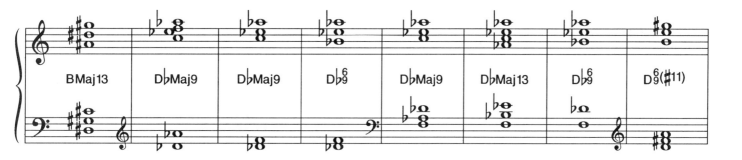

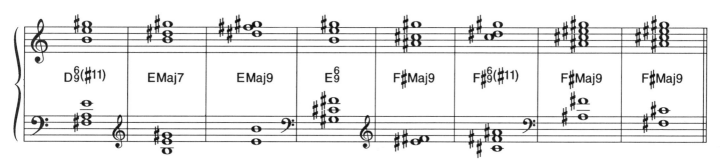

Minor Chords

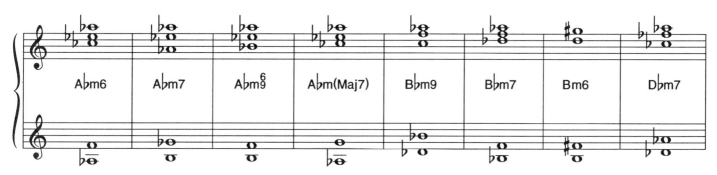

Chords-Harmonizing A♭ or G♯

D♭m9(Maj7) E♭m11 Fm7 Fm9 F♯m9 F♯m11 F♯m9(6) F♯m9

Dominant Chords

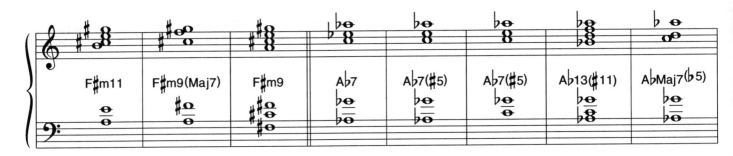

F♯m11 F♯m9(Maj7) F♯m9 A♭7 A♭7(♯5) A♭7(♯5) A♭13(♯11) A♭Maj7(♭5)

A♭13 A♭13sus A♭7(♭9) A♭7(♭9) A♭7(♯5/♯9) B♭7 B♭7(♭5) B♭9

B♭9 B♭7(♭9) B♭7(♯11) B13(♭9) B13sus B13 B13 C7(♯5/♯9)

C7(♯5) D♭7 D♭9 D♭7(♭9) D♭13 D♭7(♯9) D7(♯5/♯9♯11) D7(♯11)

92

Chords-Harmonizing A♭ or G♯

Eb9sus   E13   F7(♯9)   F7($_{\flat 9}^{\sharp 5}$)   F♯9sus   F♯13   F♯13(♯11)   F♯11

Diminished Chords

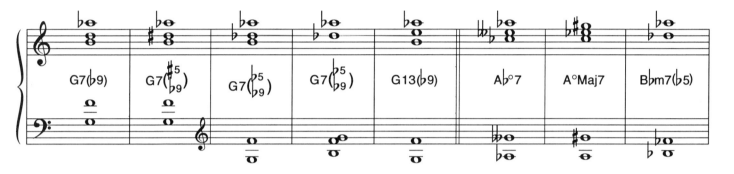

G7(♭9)   G7($_{\flat 9}^{\sharp 5}$)   G7($_{\flat 9}^{\flat 5}$)   G7($_{\flat 9}^{\flat 5}$)   G13(♭9)   A♭°7   A°Maj7   B♭m7(♭5)

Dm7(♭5)   Eb9sus(♭5)   Ebm11(♭5)   Ebm11(♭5)   Ebm11(♭5)   Fm7(♭5)   F♯m9(♭5)   G7($_{\flat 9}^{\flat 5}$)

Suspended Chords

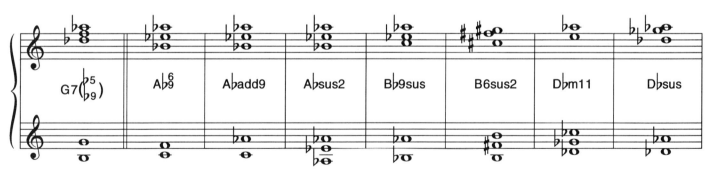

G7($_{\flat 9}^{\flat 5}$)   A♭$^{6}_{9}$ A♭add9   A♭sus2   B♭9sus   B6sus2   D♭m11   D♭sus

Ebsus   F♯9sus   A♭/B♭   A♭/G♭   D♭/A♭   D♭/C♭   E/F♯   E/B

Chords-Harmonizing A

Major Chords

AMaj7 · AMaj7(♯5) · B♭Maj7 · B♭Maj9 · B♭Maj9 · B♭Maj7 · C⁶/9 · C⁶/9(♯11)

CMaj13 · DMaj9 · DMaj9 · D⁶/9 · DMaj9 · DMaj13 · D⁶/9 · E♭⁶/9(♯11)

E♭⁶/9(♯11) · FMaj7 · FMaj9 · F⁶/9 · GMaj9 · G⁶/9(♯11) · GMaj9 · GMaj9

Minor Chords

Am6 · Am7 · Am⁶/9 · Am(Maj7) · Bm9 · Bm7 · Cm6 · Dm7

Dm7 · Dm9 · Dm7 · Dm9 · Dm11 · Dm⁶/9 · Dm9 · D9sus

94

Chords-Harmonizing A

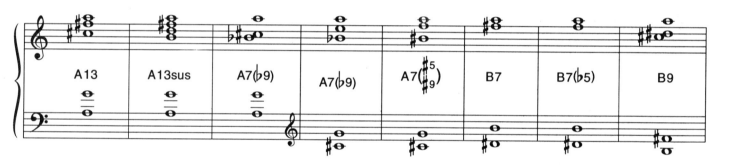

Dominant Chords

Chords-Harmonizing A

E9sus   F13   G♭7(♯9)   G♭7(♯5♭9)   G9sus   G13   G13(♯11)   G11

Diminished Chords

A♭7(♭9)   G♯7(♯5♭9)   G♯7(♭5♭9)   G♯7(♭5♭9)   G♯13(♭9)   A°7   B♭°Maj7   Bm7(♭5)

E♭m7(♭5)   E9sus(♭5)   Em11(♭5)   Em11(♭5)   Em11(♭5)   F♯m7(♭5)   Gm9(♭5)   G♯7(♭5♭9)

Suspended Chords

G♯7(♭5♭9)   A⁶₉   Aadd9   Asus2   B9sus   C6sus2   Dm11   Dsus

Esus   G9sus   A/B   A/G   D/A   D/C   F/G   F/C

96

Minor Chords

Chords-Harmonizing B♭ or A#

Major Chords

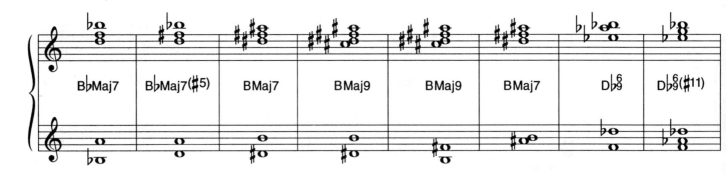

BbMaj7 | BbMaj7(#5) | BMaj7 | BMaj9 | BMaj9 | BMaj7 | Db⁶₉ | Db⁶₉(#11)

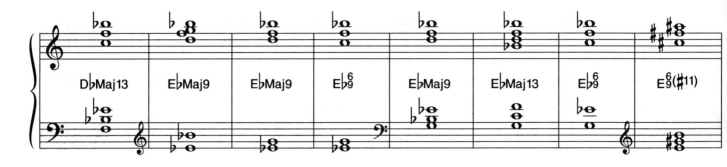

DbMaj13 | EbMaj9 | EbMaj9 | Eb⁶₉ | EbMaj9 | EbMaj13 | Eb⁶₉ | E⁶₉(#11)

E⁶₉(#11) | F#Maj7 | F#Maj9 | F#⁶₉ | AbMaj9 | Ab⁶₉(#11) | AbMaj9 | AbMaj9

Minor Chords

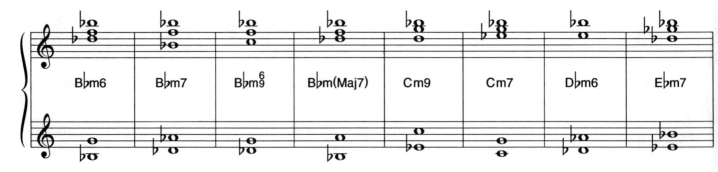

Bbm6 | Bbm7 | Bbm⁶₉ | Bbm(Maj7) | Cm9 | Cm7 | Dbm6 | Ebm7

Ebm7 | Ebm9 | Ebm7 | Ebm9 | Ebm11 | Ebm⁶₉ | Ebm9 | Eb9sus

98

Chords-Harmonizing B♭ or A♯

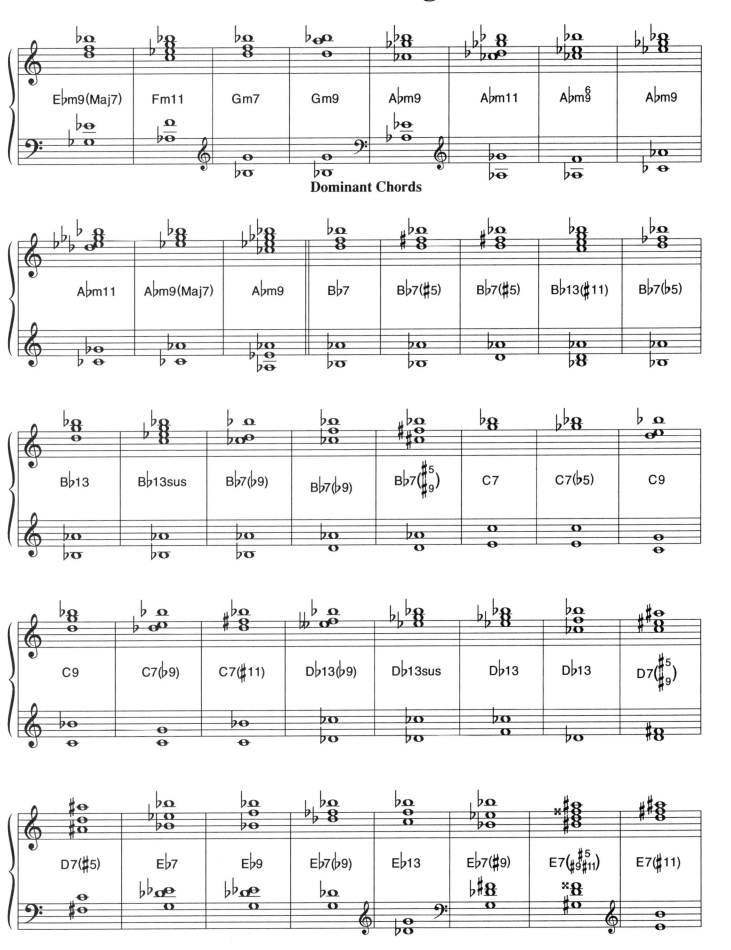

Dominant Chords

99

Major Chords

Chords-Harmonizing B or C♭

| BMaj7 | BMaj7(♯5) | CMaj7 | CMaj9 | CMaj9 | CMaj7 | D$_9^6$ | D$_9^6$(♯11) |

| DMaj13 | EMaj9 | EMaj9 | E$_9^6$ | EMaj9 | EMaj13 | E$_9^6$ | F$_9^6$(♯11) |

| F$_9^6$(♯11) | GMaj7 | GMaj9 | G$_9^6$ | AMaj9 | A$_9^6$(♯11) | AMaj9 | AMaj9 |

Minor Chords

| Bm6 | Bm7 | Bm$_9^6$ | Bm(Maj7) | D♭m9 | D♭m7 | Dm6 | Em7 |

| Em7 | Em9 | Em7 | Em9 | Em11 | Em$_9^6$ | Em9 | E9sus |

Chords-Harmonizing B or C♭

Dominant Chords

101

Chords-Harmonizing B or C♭

Quartal Harmonies-Key of C

Major Structures

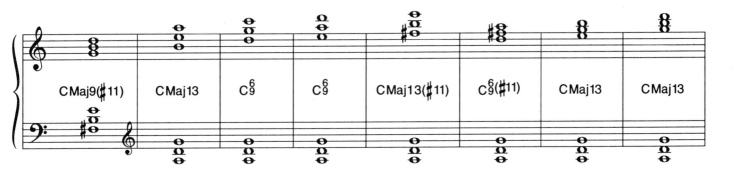

Minor Structures

Quartal Harmonies-Key of C

Row 1: Cm11(b13) · C9sus · Cm11 · Cm11(b13) · Cm11 · Cm11 · Cm11(b13) · Cm11

Row 2: Cm11 · Cm11 · Cm13 · Cm13 · Cm11(b13) · C7sus · Csus(add9) · Cm11

Row 3: Cm11(b13) · C9sus · Cm11 · Cm11(b13) · Cm7(b9 b13) · Cm11(b13) · Cm7(b5 b9 b13) · Cm7(b13)

Dominant Structures

Row 4: Cm7(b13) · Cm7(b5 b9 b13) · Cm7(b13) · C9sus · C13(b9) · C13 · C7sus · C7sus(b9 #11 b13)

Row 5: C7sus(#9 b13) · C7sus(#11) · C13sus · C7sus(#9) · C7sus(#9 #11 13) · E/C7sus · C7sus(b5 b9) · C9sus

104

Quartal Harmonies-Key of D♭

Major Structures

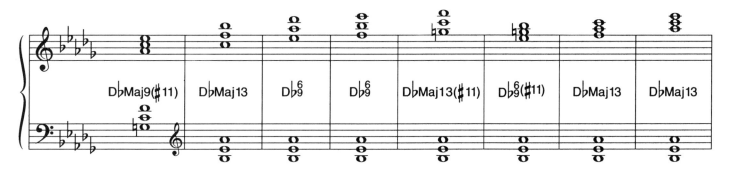

Minor Structures

Quartal Harmonies-Key of D♭

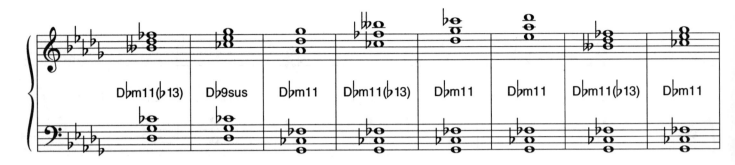

D♭m11(♭13)   D♭9sus   D♭m11   D♭m11(♭13)   D♭m11   D♭m11   D♭m11(♭13)   D♭m11

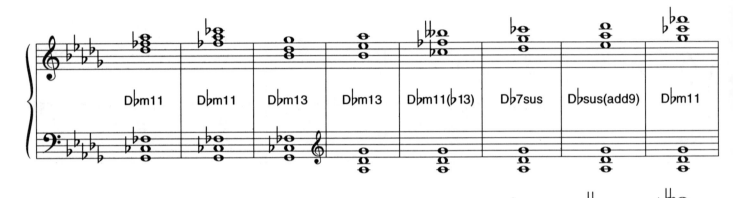

D♭m11   D♭m11   D♭m13   D♭m13   D♭m11(♭13)   D♭7sus   D♭sus(add9)   D♭m11

D♭m11(♭13)   D♭9sus   D♭m11   D♭m11(♭13)   D♭m7($^{♭9}_{♭13}$)   D♭m11(♭13)   D♭m7($^{♭5}_{♭9♭13}$)   D♭m7(♭13)

Dominant Structures

D♭m7(♭13)   D♭m7($^{♭5}_{♭9♭13}$)   D♭m7(♭13)   D♭9sus   D♭13(♭9)   D♭13   D♭7sus   D♭7sus($^{♭9}_{♯11♭13}$)

D♭7sus($^{♯9}_{♭13}$)   D♭7sus(♯11)   D♭13sus   D♭7sus(♯9)   D♭7sus($^{♯9}_{♯11♯13}$)   F/D♭7sus   D♭7sus($^{♭5}_{♭9}$)   D♭9sus

Quartal Harmonies-Key of D

Major Structures

D_9^6 | DMaj9(#11) | D_9^6 | DMaj13 | $D_9^{6(#11)}$ | DMaj9 | D_9^6 | DMaj13(#11)

D_9^6 | DMaj13 | $D_9^{6(#11)}$ | DMaj13 | DMaj13(#11) | DMaj13(#11) | DMaj13(#11) | DMaj13(#11)

DMaj9(#11) | DMaj13 | D_9^6 | D_9^6 | DMaj13(#11) | $D_9^{6(#11)}$ | DMaj13 | DMaj13

D_9^6 | DMaj13 | DMaj13 | DMaj13(#11) | DMaj13 | DMaj13 | DMaj13(#11) | DMaj13

Minor Structures

DMaj13 | DMaj13(b9) | Dm11($_{b13}^{b9}$) | Dm11 | Dm11 | D7sus($_{#11 b13}^{b9}$) | Dm11(b13) | Dm11

Quartal Harmonies-Key of D

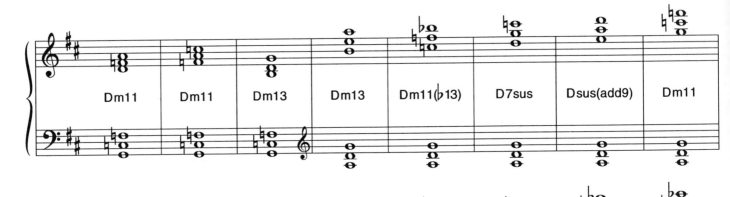

Quartal Harmonies-Key of E♭

Major Structures

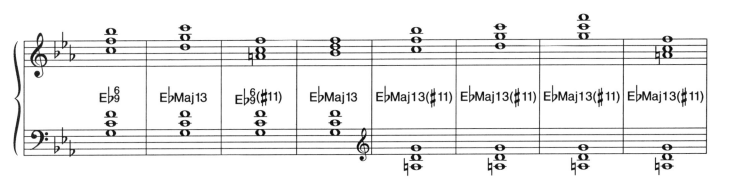

Minor Structures

Quartal Harmonies-Key of E♭

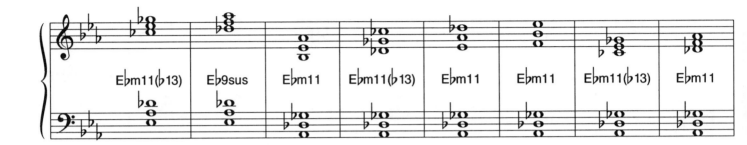

| E♭m11(♭13) | E♭9sus | E♭m11 | E♭m11(♭13) | E♭m11 | E♭m11 | E♭m11(♭13) | E♭m11 |

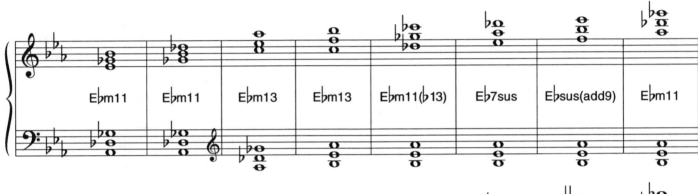

| E♭m11 | E♭m11 | E♭m13 | E♭m13 | E♭m11(♭13) | E♭7sus | E♭sus(add9) | E♭m11 |

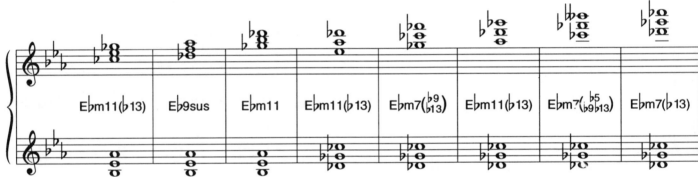

| E♭m11(♭13) | E♭9sus | E♭m11 | E♭m11(♭13) | E♭m7(♭9 ♭13) | E♭m11(♭13) | E♭m7(♭5 ♭9♭13) | E♭m7(♭13) |

Dominant Structures

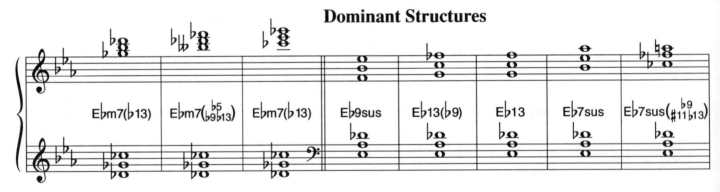

| E♭m7(♭13) | E♭m7(♭5 ♭9♭13) | E♭m7(♭13) | E♭9sus | E♭13(♭9) | E♭13 | E♭7sus | E♭7sus(♭9 #11♭13) |

| E♭7sus(#9 ♭13) | E♭7sus(#11) | E♭13sus | E♭7sus(#9) | E♭7sus(#9 #11#13) | G/E♭7sus | E♭7sus(♭5 ♭9) | E♭9sus |

Quartal Harmonies-Key of E

Major Structures

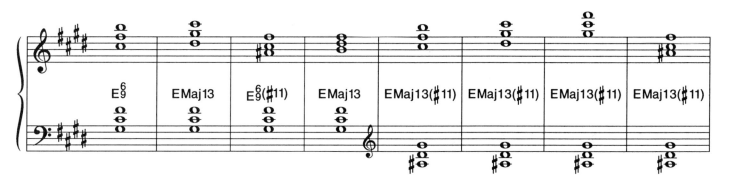

Minor Structures

Quartal Harmonies-Key of E

| Em11(b13) | E9sus | Em11 | Em11(b13) | Em11 | Em11 | Em11(b13) | Em11 |

| Em11 | Em11 | Em13 | Em13 | Em11(b13) | E7sus | Esus(add9) | Em11 |

| Em11(b13) | E9sus | Em11 | Em11(b13) | Em7(b9 b13) | Em11(b13) | Em7(b9 b5 13) | Em7(b13) |

Dominant Structures

| Em7(b13) | Em7(b9 b5 13) | Em7(b13) | E9sus | E13(b9) | E13 | E7sus | E7sus(#9 #11 b13) |

| E7sus(#9 b13) | E7sus(#11) | E13sus | E7sus(#9) | E7sus(#9 #11 13) | G#/E7sus | E7sus(b5 b9) | E9sus |

112

Quartal Harmonies-Key of F

Major Structures

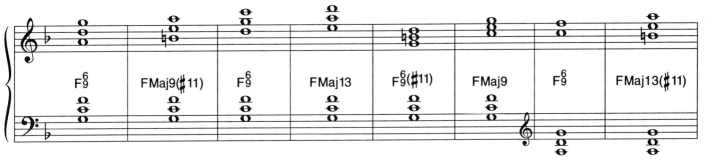

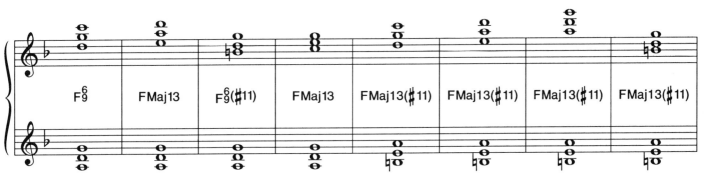

Minor Structures

113

Quartal Harmonies-Key of F

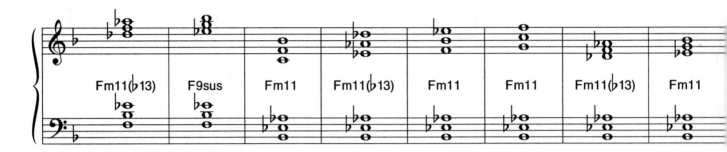

Fm11(♭13) F9sus Fm11 Fm11(♭13) Fm11 Fm11 Fm11(♭13) Fm11

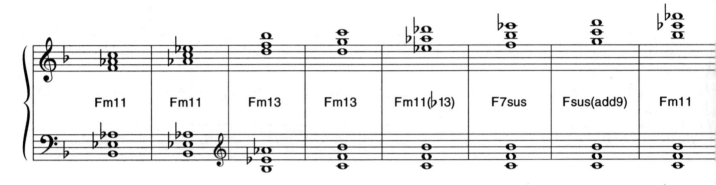

Fm11 Fm11 Fm13 Fm13 Fm11(♭13) F7sus Fsus(add9) Fm11

Fm11(♭13) F9sus Fm11 Fm11(♭13) Fm7(♭9♭13) Fm11(♭13) Fm7(♭5♭9♭13) Fm7(♭13)

Dominant Structures

Fm7(♭13) Fm7(♭5♭9♭13) Fm7(♭13) F9sus F13(♭9) F13 F7sus F7sus(♯11♭9♭13)

F7sus(♯9♭13) F7sus(♯11) F13sus F7sus(♯9) F7sus(♯9♯11♯13) A/F7sus F7sus(♭5♭9) F9sus

Quartal Harmonies-Key of G♭

Major Structures

Minor Structures

Quartal Harmonies-Key of G♭

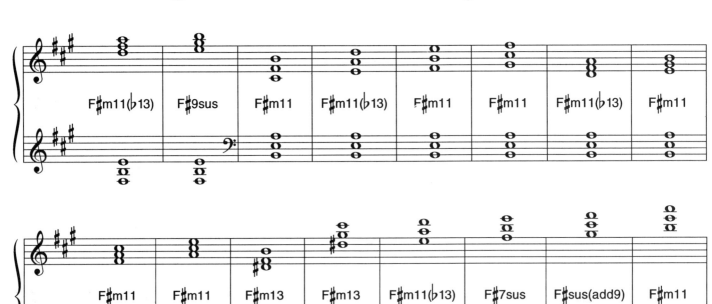

F♯m11(♭13) | F♯9sus | F♯m11 | F♯m11(♭13) | F♯m11 | F♯m11 | F♯m11(♭13) | F♯m11

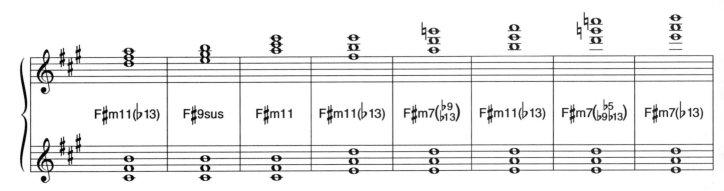

F♯m11 | F♯m11 | F♯m13 | F♯m13 | F♯m11(♭13) | F♯7sus | F♯sus(add9) | F♯m11

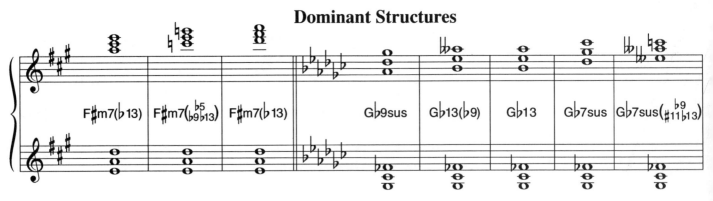

F♯m11(♭13) | F♯9sus | F♯m11 | F♯m11(♭13) | F♯m7(♭9♭13) | F♯m11(♭13) | F♯m7(♭5♭9♭13) | F♯m7(♭13)

Dominant Structures

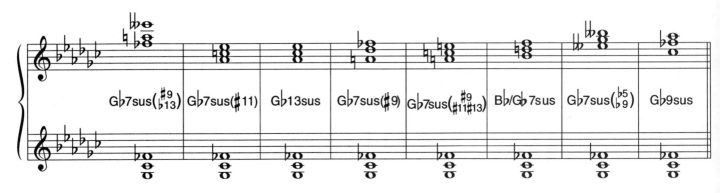

F♯m7(♭13) | F♯m7(♭5♭9♭13) | F♯m7(♭13) | G♭9sus | G♭13(♭9) | G♭13 | G♭7sus | G♭7sus(♯11♭9♭13)

G♭7sus(♯9♭13) | G♭7sus(♯11) | G♭13sus | G♭7sus(♯9) | G♭7sus(♯9♯11♭13) | B♭/G♭7sus | G♭7sus(♭5♭9) | G♭9sus

Quartal Harmonies-Key of G

Major Structures

Chords (row 1): G$^6_9$, GMaj9($\sharp$11), G$^6_9$, GMaj13, G$^6_9$($\sharp$11), GMaj9, G$^6_9$, GMaj13($\sharp$11)

Chords (row 2): G$^6_9$, GMaj13, G$^6_9$($\sharp$11), GMaj13, GMaj13($\sharp$11), GMaj13($\sharp$11), GMaj13($\sharp$11), GMaj13($\sharp$11)

Chords (row 3): GMaj9($\sharp$11), GMaj13, G$^6_9$, G$^6_9$, GMaj13($\sharp$11), G$^6_9$($\sharp$11), GMaj13, GMaj13

Chords (row 4): G$^6_9$, GMaj13, GMaj13, GMaj13($\sharp$11), GMaj13, GMaj13, GMaj13($\sharp$11), GMaj13

Minor Structures

Chords (row 5): GMaj13, GMaj13($\flat$9), Gm11($^{\flat9}_{\flat13}$), Gm11, Gm11, G7sus($^{\flat9}_{\sharp11\flat13}$), Gm11($\flat$13), Gm11

117

Quartal Harmonies-Key of G

Row 1 chords: Gm11(b13), G9sus, Gm11, Gm11(b13), Gm11, Gm11, Gm11(b13), Gm11

Row 2 chords: Gm11, Gm11, Gm13, Gm13, Gm11(b13), G7sus, Gsus(add9), Gm11

Row 3 chords: Gm11(b13), G9sus, Gm11, Gm11(b13), Gm7(b9/b13), Gm11(b13), Gm7(b9/b5/13), Gm7(b13)

Dominant Structures

Row 4 chords: Gm7(b13), Gm7(b5/b9/b13), Gm7(b13), G9sus, G13(b9), G13, G7sus, G7sus(b9/#11/b13)

Row 5 chords: G7sus(#9/b13), G7sus(#11), G13sus, G7sus(#9), G7sus(#9/#11/#13), B/G7sus, G7sus(b5/b9), G9sus

Quartal Harmonies-Key of A♭

Major Structures

Minor Structures

Quartal Harmonies-Key of A♭

Row 1 chords: Abm11(b13) | Ab9sus | Abm11 | Abm11(b13) | Abm11 | Abm11 | Abm11(b13) | Abm11

Row 2 chords: Abm11 | Abm11 | Abm13 | Abm13 | Abm11(b13) | Ab7sus | Absus(add9) | Abm11

Row 3 chords: Abm11(b13) | Ab9sus | Abm11 | Abm11(b13) | Abm7(b9 b13) | Abm11(b13) | Abm7(b9 b5 13) | Abm7(b13)

Dominant Structures

Row 4 chords: Abm7(b13) | Abm7(b5 b9 b13) | Abm7(b13) | Ab9sus | Ab13(b9) | Ab13 | Ab7sus | Ab7sus(#11 b9 13)

Row 5 chords: Ab7sus(#9 b13) | Ab7sus(#11) | Ab13sus | Ab7sus(#9) | Ab7sus(#9 #11 #13) | C/Ab7sus | Ab7sus(b5 b9) | Ab9sus

Quartal Harmonies-Key of A

Major Structures

Minor Structures

121

Quartal Harmonies-Key of A

(Row 1) Am11(♭13) | A9sus | Am11 | Am11(♭13) | Am11 | Am11 | Am11(♭13) | Am11

(Row 2) Am11 | Am11 | Am13 | Am13 | Am11(♭13) | A7sus | Asus(add9) | Am11

(Row 3) Am11(♭13) | A9sus | Am11 | Am11(♭13) | Am7(♭9♭13) | Am11(♭13) | Am7(♭9♭5♭13) | Am7(♭13)

Dominant Structures

(Row 4) Am7(♭13) | Am7(♭9♭5♭13) | Am7(♭13) | A9sus | A13(♭9) | A13 | A7sus | A7sus(♯11♭9♭13)

(Row 5) A7sus(♯9♭13) | A7sus(♯11) | A13sus | A7sus(♯9) | A7sus(♯11♭9♭13) | C♯/A7sus | A7sus(♭5♭9) | A9sus

122

Quartal Harmonies-Key of B♭

Major Structures

Row 1: B♭⁶/₉ | B♭Maj9(♯11) | B♭⁶/₉ | B♭Maj13 | B♭⁶/₉(♯11) | B♭Maj9 | B♭⁶/₉ | B♭Maj13(♯11)

Row 2: B♭⁶/₉ | B♭Maj13 | B♭⁶/₉(♯11) | B♭Maj13 | B♭Maj13(♯11) | B♭Maj13(♯11) | B♭Maj13(♯11) | B♭Maj13(♯11)

Row 3: B♭Maj9(♯11) | B♭Maj13 | B♭⁶/₉ | B♭⁶/₉ | B♭Maj13(♯11) | B♭⁶/₉(♯11) | B♭Maj13 | B♭Maj13

Row 4: B♭⁶/₉ | B♭Maj13 | B♭Maj13 | B♭Maj13(♯11) | B♭Maj13 | B♭Maj13 | B♭Maj13(♯11) | B♭Maj13

Minor Structures

Row 5: B♭Maj13 | B♭Maj13(♭9) | B♭m11(♭9♭13) | B♭m11 | B♭m11 | B♭7sus(♭9♯11♭13) | B♭m11(♭13) | B♭m11

123

Quartal Harmonies-Key of B♭

Bbm11(b13) | Bb9sus | Bbm11 | Bbm11(b13) | Bbm11 | Bbm11 | Bbm11(b13) | Bbm11

Bbm11 | Bbm11 | Bbm13 | Bbm13 | Bbm11(b13) | Bb7sus | Bbsus(add9) | Bbm11

Bbm11(b13) | Bb9sus | Bbm11 | Bbm11(b13) | Bbm7(b9 b13) | Bbm11(b13) | Bbm7(b5 b9 b13) | Bbm7(b13)

Dominant Structures

Bbm7(b13) | Bbm7(b5 b9 b13) | Bbm7(b13) | Bb9sus | Bb13(b9) | Bb13 | Bb7sus | Bb7sus(#11 b9 b13)

Bb7sus(#9 b13) | Bb7sus(#11) | Bb13sus | Bb7sus(#9) | Bb7sus(#9 #11 #13) | D/Bb 7sus | Bb7sus(b5 b9) | Bb9sus

124

Quartal Harmonies-Key of B

Major Structures

B$^6_9$ BMaj9($\sharp$11)   B$^6_9$ BMaj13   B$^{6}_{9}$($\sharp$11)   BMaj9   B$^6_9$ BMaj13($\sharp$11)

B$^6_9$ BMaj13   B$^{6}_{9}$($\sharp$11)   BMaj13   BMaj13($\sharp$11)   BMaj13($\sharp$11)   BMaj13($\sharp$11)   BMaj13($\sharp$11)

BMaj9($\sharp$11)   BMaj13   B$^6_9$ B$^6_9$ BMaj13($\sharp$11)   B$^{6}_{9}$($\sharp$11)   BMaj13   BMaj13

B$^6_9$ BMaj13   BMaj13   BMaj13($\sharp$11)   BMaj13   BMaj13   BMaj13($\sharp$11)   BMaj13

Minor Structures

BMaj13   BMaj13($\flat$9)   Bm11($^{\flat9}_{\flat13}$)   Bm11   Bm11   B7sus($^{\flat9}_{\sharp11\flat13}$)   Bm11($\flat$13)   Bm11

125

Quartal Harmonies-Key of B

Bm11(♭13) B9sus Bm11 Bm11(♭13) Bm11 Bm11 Bm11(♭13) Bm11

Bm11 Bm11 Bm13 Bm13 Bm11(♭13) B7sus Bsus(add9) Bm11

Bm11(♭13) B9sus Bm11 Bm11(♭13) Bm7(♭9♭13) Bm11(♭13) Bm7(♭9♭5♭13) Bm7(♭13)

Dominant Structures

Bm7(♭13) Bm7(♭9♭5♭13) Bm7(♭13) B9sus B13(♭9) B13 B7sus B7sus(♯11♭9♭13)

B7sus(♯9♭13) B7sus(♯11) B13sus B7sus(♯9) B7sus(♯9♯11♯13) D♯/B7sus B7sus(♭9♭5) B9sus

126

Spelling Suggestions

Many chord symbols acquired a number of different spellings as the theory for jazz chords has developed. While today most of the chord names are agreed upon, occasionally different ways of writing of the same chord may appear. Below are some possibilities of different chord spellings:

$C = CMA = C\Delta = CM7 = Cma7 = CMA7 = Cmaj7 = C\Delta7$ and even $C7$, when usually $C7$ refers to a Mm7

$CM9 = Cma7(9)$, however $C9$ is always a Dominant chord

$C = C$ min

$C7-5 = C7-5 = C7m5 = C^{\emptyset} = C^{\emptyset}7 = Chalfdim7$

$Cdim7 = C^{\circ}$

$C69 = C6$ add 9

$C7$ aug5 $= C7+5 = C7\sharp5 = Caug7 = C+7 = C7+$

$Cma7(-3) = CM7m3 = Cm(Maj7) = CmM7 = Cm\sharp7$

$C7\sharp9 = C7+9 = C9+$

Comit 3 = Cno3 refers specifically to avoiding the 3rd either because of conflicting notes in other instruments or to leave the sound more open and vulnerable, as in open Major-minor system to be discussed later.

Chords can also be spelled differently due to the fact that 2nd of the chord is the same note as the 9th, 4th is the same note as the 11th, and 6th is the same as 13th. The difference is determined by the voice leading and the place of the note in the chord. For example D in C11 chord is below the 7th, therefore it should be the 2nd, or a sus chord. However, when D is above the 7th it should be called the 9th.

$Cmin11 = Csus9$, except for the questionable E$\flat$ in the chord.

Cadd 9 usually refers to $C9$ with no 7th, Cadd 13 usually refers to $C9$ with no 9th or 11th.

$Cadd13 = C13$ no11 no 9

$Csus2 = C(add9)$

About the Author

Misha V. Stefanuk started playing piano when he was 5. He studied at Moscow Conservatory School, Russian Academy of Music, Moscow Studio of Music Improvisation Art, Belmont University and Washington State University. He has written more than 80 opuses for a variety of instrumentations. His credits include original music for more than 20 theater productions and about 30 videos, including the platinum Y2K Survival Guide with Leonard Nimoy. Amongst his other compositions is The Jazz Piano Album published by Mel Bay. Mr. Stefanuk is a prize winner of "Stereotypes and Nations" Composition Competition held by Muzica Centrum Art Society in Krakow, Poland for his Composition Equinokse for oboe, string trio, and prepared piano; Concerto-Aria Composition Competition at Belmont University for his The New American Symphony; Outstanding Piano Player at 129th Annual Lionel Hampton Jazz Festival, winning a Kurzweil Mark V digital piano and full scholarships at Belmont University, Washington State University and Skidmore Summer Jazz Institute.